✔ KU-256-046

This is my mother,
Tammy Wynette...

Long before Mom died, I began to think about writing a book about her. [Her own] autobiography began in the fields and ended on the mountaintop. My story spirals back into the depths, and not a day has passed since I began this work that I have not regretted that the Tammy Wynette projected through my eyes is not an altogether joyous vision. Yet, I was bound to tell the story that had to be told . . .

"Tammy Wynette's April 6, 1998, death was a shock. An even greater shock came when her daughters demanded an autopsy in 1999. What did Daly and her siblings hope to discover? The whole story of Tammy's demise has not been told. Daly relates what she knows, what she suspects, and how it all fits together. Tammy Wynette was an American icon, far more complex than the 'Stand by Your Man' image casual fans saw."

—*Kirkus Reviews*

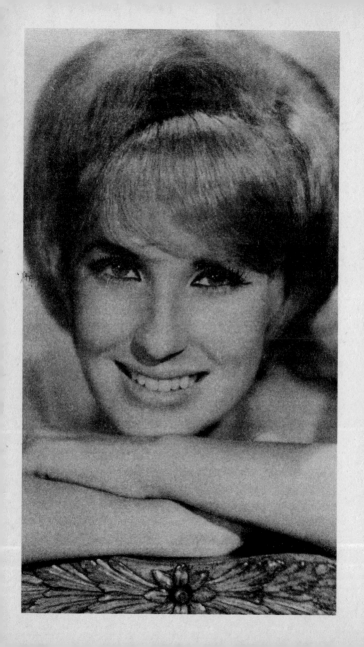

Tammy Wynette

A DAUGHTER RECALLS
HER MOTHER'S TRAGIC
LIFE AND DEATH

Jackie Daly
with Tom Carter

BERKLEY BOULEVARD BOOKS, NEW YORK

If you purchased this book without a cover, you should be aware that this book is stolen property. It was reported as "unsold and destroyed" to the publisher, and neither the author nor the publisher has received any payment for this "stripped book."

The authors gratefully acknowledge permission to quote from the following:

"Dear Daughters," words and music by Tammy Wynette, © 1977 Universal—MCA Music Publishing Inc., a division of Universal Studios. International copyright secured. All rights reserved. Used by permission.

"Stand by Your Man," Tammy Wynette and Billy Sherrill, © 1968 (Renewed) EMI Gallico Music Corp. All rights reserved. Used by permission. Warner Bros. Publications U.S. Inc., Miami, FL 33014.

TAMMY WYNETTE:
A DAUGHTER RECALLS HER MOTHER'S
TRAGIC LIFE AND DEATH

A Berkley Boulevard Book / published by arrangement with the author

PRINTING HISTORY
G. P. Putnam's Sons hardcover edition / May 2000
Berkley Boulevard edition / April 2001

All rights reserved.
Copyright © 2000 by Jackie Daly and Manor Publications, Inc.
Book design by Jennifer Ann Daddio.
Cover design by Isabella Fasciano.
Cover photograph © Paul Natkin/Outline.
This book, or parts thereof, may not be reproduced in any form without permission. For information address: The Berkley Publishing Group, a division of Penguin Putnam Inc., 375 Hudson Street, New York, New York 10014.

The Penguin Putnam Inc. World Wide Web site address is
http://www.penguinputnam.com

ISBN: 0-425-17925-7

BERKLEY BOULEVARD
Berkley Boulevard Books are published by
The Berkley Publishing Group,
a division of Penguin Putnam Inc., 375 Hudson Street,
New York, New York 10014.
BERKLEY BOULEVARD and its logo
are trademarks belonging to Penguin Putnam Inc.

PRINTED IN THE UNITED STATES OF AMERICA

10 9 8 7 6 5 4 3 2 1

Acknowledgments

I WANT TO thank Mrs. George (Nancy) Jones for introducing me to members of the New York literary community, such as Mel Berger and Dean Williamson, who put this project together, and to Tom Carter, who tirelessly listened to me and helped put it all together.

Martha Dettwiller was Mom's friend for a quarter of a century and has been a surrogate mother to me the entire time. She has held my hand when I needed the support, and has held me in her arms when I have wept. No one could have a better friend, and no one was a better friend to this project.

Special thanks to Grace McDaniel and Leta Cook for their friendship and support.

Susie Reed and Jim Henderson were tireless researchers. They did whatever they were asked to do, and never uttered one syllable of dissent.

Dan Warlick and Ed Yarbrough have been capable legal counsel during a very trying period of my life.

Gwen Nichols, Georgette Smith and Tina Jones, my sisters, heartily encouraged this book and gave incessant support. Sophia Paule, Kristina Paule, Natalie Paule, and Catherine Paule, my four daughters, were always patient with an absentee mother struggling to write her first book.

Janice Dale, you're the best.

Finally, I will forever be indebted to Mom's countless fans who loved her music and who loved her as a human being. I thank them for recognizing, and for occasionally forgiving, her frailties. Her life is over, but her music and memory are alive because of those wonderful people.

For my mother

PART ONE

The Long Salute

Author's Note

LONG BEFORE MOM died, I began to think about writing a book about her. She had published her autobiography in 1979, when she was only thirty-seven years old and at the peak of her career, but as time passed, and fragments of her life were filtered—often with gross distortion—through the headlines and tabloids, I wanted people to know the Tammy Wynette that I knew, to see her, for better or worse, through my eyes.

Her own account of her life, I felt, was incomplete. It was half a life and there was much to say in a sequel, but I don't think she had intentions of continuing the story herself. Her emotions and energy had been drained by health problems, by a river of painkilling fluids, by a fifth marriage she often said she wanted to end, and by the struggle to preserve her career at a time when the whiz-kid executives of country music were turning their backs on everyone over the age of forty.

Someone else would have to write the ending. I decided

to take on the task because I want people to know the rest of the story and because I also wanted to know it. I was still a teenager when *Stand by Your Man* was published, but not long afterward my life began to diverge from hers as I married, bore children and had my own nest to build.

Her book spanned what would seem to have been her most difficult and interesting years—overcoming a rural childhood that promised only a limited future and getting a toehold in professional singing, four turbulent marriages, fame, success and wealth beyond anything she could have imagined when she first started knocking on doors of Music Row. I know now that book truly was merely a beginning and her post-autobiography years were equally remarkable and absorbing, though not for the reasons I would have preferred.

That book concluded with her fifth wedding, one that, as far I knew, held the promise of bringing the happiness that had always eluded her. I left home a few years later, and while we remained in close contact, I realized there were things going on in her life that I wasn't aware of, except from secondhand accounts or from newspaper stories: the mysterious kidnapping, the bankruptcy, the endless string of surgeries, her astonishingly successful foray into pop music with a zany British group called KLF, and her aborted treatment at the Betty Ford Center, to name a few.

Writing a book about her would be a journey of discovery, an opportunity to talk with her in detail about her life in the years after the autobiography, and it would be a reason to talk with her close friends, most of whom were also close friends of mine, to get details about incidents I had not had a chance to witness.

Mom had no objections to my writing a book; during the few discussions we had about it, she offered only encouragement. I knew from the outset it would not be easy, for hers was no ordinary life.

In researching this book, I found out things that were not particularly pleasant, things there had been no need for me to know and certainly not for the whole world to know. But she was my mother and nothing I have learned in this process has diminished my love for her.

I have always felt close to Mom—even during the periods when, as a child and a teenager, I resented her frequent absences; even as an adult when we had falling-outs and went for weeks without speaking, and sometimes without seeing each other. At the same time, I felt strangely apart from her.

There was no doubt that she loved her four daughters, but she was a woman driven in many directions. She wanted simple things—a home, a husband, children—but her other longings were poison to such simplicity. She craved the road, the stage, the spotlight, the recording studio and the financial rewards of those pursuits.

Her trek from the bottomland cotton fields of Alabama to the mountaintop of country music attested to her enormous strength, but her addiction to prescription drugs and her knack for picking the wrong husbands were profound weaknesses.

On one side of her nature was a will hard enough to bulldoze the walls that Nashville had placed in the paths of "girl singers," while on another side was a sense of insecurity that ran so deep, she could never quite grasp her true stature in the music world.

Mostly, to me and my sisters, she was just Mom. When she was not touring or recording, she seemed no different from our friends' mothers. Wearing jeans, a cotton shirt and a bandanna, she would take us bowling or shopping or to a hamburger joint. She would play with us in the back-yard and cook up huge amounts of the Southern foods we all loved: biscuits and sausage with gravy for breakfast; ham and dumplings and cornbread and bread pudding for dinner.

Unfortunately, those times were rarer than I would have liked, and it took more years than it should have for me to understand who she really was. I had seen her on television, of course, and I knew that whenever her bus pulled out of the driveway she would spend the next several days performing for large audiences, but it wasn't until I was a teenager that I began to understand the dimensions of her celebrity.

When I was about fourteen, I invited a friend over after school, and seeing the photographs and other memorabilia on the walls, she blurted out, "Your mom's Tammy Wynette!" I said something like, "Uh-huh. Want a Coke?"

A year or so later when I was in high school, I was looking through a new edition of *Who's Who,* and near the back of the book I was almost startled at seeing the entry: TAMMY WYNETTE. I read through the tiny type and abbreviations and thought, *Wow, Mom really is famous.*

Even with that bit of enlightenment, I went through the next two decades not fully knowing what that celebrity meant, and it wasn't until after Mom had died—the day of her funeral, in fact—that I began to comprehend fully her impact on the people who were touched by her music.

A private service was held at Judson Baptist Church, a block from her house on Franklin Road, and afterward we all loaded into our cars to drive downtown for a public memorial service at the Ryman Auditorium, the original home of the Grand Ole Opry and still something of a country-music cathedral. I rode in a van with Nanette Crafton, who had been Mom's hairdresser and one of her closest friends for more than twenty years.

As we pulled out of the church parking lot and crept along the boulevard through a neighborhood called Melrose, I was staring blankly ahead, in my own personal fog. It was a cold, overcast day. The wind gusted hard enough to rock the van. There was no oncoming traffic, just the stream of cars headed toward the misty, distant skyline.

Suddenly, I saw up ahead a solitary figure standing in the middle of Franklin Road. As we drew nearer, I could make out an elderly black man dressed in a white shirt and dark slacks, his right arm raised and bent into a crisp salute. He stood there, as straight and rigid as a flagpole, and held his salute until our procession had passed. For the first time in days, I smiled and felt a comforting warmth pass through me. *He probably didn't even know Mom,* I thought. *Probably didn't even know OF her.*

Probably I was wrong.

When we arrived at the Ryman, I was jolted by another scene. The streets were lined with television satellite broadcast trucks and the queue of visitors trying to get inside snaked all the way around the old theater. Thousands came, some arriving early in the morning, hoping to get one of the 2,200 seats, and, I would learn later, millions more around the world watched on television.

CNN was broadcasting the memorial live, and for the first time since the death of Princess Di, the BBC also suspended its regular broadcasting to give two hours to the service.

The scope of that outpouring made me more determined than ever to proceed with this book.

It would not, however, be the volume I had originally anticipated. Almost from the moment Mom died, events began to crowd their way into my own schemes. The odd circumstance of her death, the simple questions that never got answered, the inexplicable behavior of official Nashville, the polarization of the country-music community—all of these and more conspired to take control of this book and give it a direction I could not have foreseen.

The hope that has propelled me in the year and a half since her crypt was sealed is that the many mysteries surrounding my mother's death can ultimately be resolved—although, perhaps, they never will. Some of the vital facts have already been lost forever, under circumstances that have been questioned. Some of the facts have only been uncovered through dogged persistence and investigation, often in the face of official indifference or inaction. Others are still hidden, or are subject to ongoing legal dispute.

I am not able to finally resolve the many questions that to this day remain unanswered. What I can do in these pages is present all of the available facts as I best have come to know them—facts that have led me, my sisters and many others to conclude that my mother did not have to die on that dark Monday in April of 1998.

My mother's autobiography began in the fields and ended on the mountaintop. My story spirals back into the depths, and not a day has passed since I began this work that I have not regretted that the Tammy Wynette projected through my eyes is not an altogether joyful vision. Yet, I was bound to tell the story that had to be told.

One

I KNEW WHEN I woke up that morning that it was not going to be a very happy day. My husband, Larry, was coming up to Nashville from Florida with divorce papers for me to sign.

Our parting had not been acrimonious and we remained friends, but after two years of separation we had decided that reconciliation was out of the question and there was no reason to prolong the legal bond between us. Still, officially ending a marriage is rarely a joyous occasion.

Larry's flight was to arrive early in the afternoon and I had taken the day off work so I could pick him up at the airport and spend a little time with him before he went back home.

Mom had called a day or two earlier and asked me to stop by when I had a chance. I was planning to take my daughters to Disney World during spring break, and she wanted to give me some money for the trip. Since I hadn't seen her in a few days, I decided to stop by before meeting

Larry. Her health had really begun to worry me. She was so thin and frail and she seemed to sleep all the time.

She and Richey—her husband's name was George Richardson, but ever since he moved to Nashville he had used the surname Richey and that's what everyone called him; not George, just Richey—lived on Franklin Road about a five-minute drive from my apartment in Brentwood, so it was easy enough for me to check on her a couple of times a week.

Sometimes she would call me at work and invite me to stop by on my way home to pick up food she had prepared for me and my four daughters. She loved cooking for people and I appreciated her efforts, but I had even begun to dread going to her house because her condition depressed me so much.

That Monday, I stopped by about noon and wasn't surprised to find Mom asleep. She was lying on a couch, on her side, with her legs pulled up in front of her and covered by a blanket. Usually, when someone came into the house while Mom was napping, the sound of footsteps on the tile floor would wake her enough that she would open an eye or make some gesture to acknowledge them.

That day, she didn't stir.

Richey was sitting on another sofa facing her and he was barely awake. He was wearing a bathrobe that hung open. The television was on, but neither of them was watching it. I felt a quick stab of impatience. *What is the matter with them?* I thought. *They sleep fifteen hours a day.*

When I tried to make conversation with Richey, his eyes opened only halfway.

It didn't make sense. Some days when I came by, Mom seemed as normal as I could expect, considering her medical history. She would be out in her garden or in the kitchen cooking up a storm or getting dressed for a shopping trip. The next day she might be crashed on the sofa, unable to sit up.

This was one of those days. Watching her lying motionless on the couch, I remembered that a week before she had been energetic enough to throw a baby shower for Karen Sloas, one of her backup singers, and she'd looked better than I had seen her in a long time. Now she couldn't lift an eyelid.

Richey wasn't in much better shape. After a few minutes of trying to talk to him, I gave up.

"Tell Mom I came by," I said, heading toward the door.

He grunted, "Uh-huh."

LARRY AND I talked for a long time that afternoon before he got the divorce papers from his bag and handed them to me. I looked them over quickly, attached my signature and gave them back to him. It was done, and I think I may have felt a slight relief. We changed clothes and drove over to Hillsboro Village, to a nice restaurant called The Trace.

On the drive back to my place, it occurred to me that despite the unpleasant purpose of my soon-to-be exhusband's visit, the day had not been quite the downer I had expected. In fact, the brief visit to my mother's house had upset me more than anything that passed between Larry and me.

We arrived home about nine-thirty, and, as I always do when I have been gone even for a few minutes, I went straight to the phone and dialed the Call Notes number to check my messages.

The automated voice said, "You have thirteen new messages."

My first thought was *Oh, man, I must be pretty important today.* At the same time, I felt a sense of foreboding. I never have that many messages. I sat down at the dining table and pressed the "one" button. The machine told me the message was received at seven-thirty, and the next voice I heard was that of my sister Gwen.

"Jackie, you need to call Mom's house," she said. "Something's happened."

My heart sank. Without listening to the other messages, I hung up and dialed Mom's house. Sylvia Richardson answered. She was Richey's ex–sister-in-law. Even after she divorced his brother Paul, she had stayed on as Richey's secretary.

"You need to come over," she said.

"What's wrong, Sylvia?"

"Your mom has passed away," she said.

Larry knew something bad had happened. He came over to me. I dropped my head to the table.

"Mom's dead," I told him, and handed him the phone.

He talked to Sylvia for just a few seconds, and we left the apartment so fast that I'm not sure I bothered to lock the door behind us.

There were a lot of cars at Mom's house and some people standing around outside. Doug Anderson, a Nashville police officer who sometimes worked security for Mom in his off-duty hours, was out front talking with Mike Martinovich, who did marketing and publicity for CBS, her record label.

"I'm sorry," Mike said, giving me a quick hug before Larry and I went inside.

Richey's office was down the hall on the left and we could hear him sobbing and wailing as we went toward a sitting area just off the kitchen, where Mom seemed to have spent most of her time lately. Gwen and Tina, another of my sisters, were there, along with most of Richey's family. I remember seeing his niece, Sandy, his brother Paul and, of course, Sylvia. There may have been a dozen others in the house, some of whom I didn't know.

Tina was sitting at one end of the couch beside a mound of blankets. I was horrified when I realized she was rubbing my mother's feet.

My mother was lying there, on the same sofa where she had been when I visited ten hours earlier. Gwen had called at seven-thirty, so I assumed Mom had died before that. Now it was past nine-thirty and I couldn't understand why her body was still here, still lying where she had died, left like some kind of centerpiece for a ghoulish gathering.

The blood rushed to my head and, suddenly, everything was surreal: Richey's moans wafting down the hall; blurred figures moving in and out of the kitchen, drinking coffee, smoking cigarettes and talking in muffled voices; the constant metallic toll of the telephone; my dead mother curled into a fetal position facing the back of the sofa and the catheter used for administering painkillers and intravenous feeding bulging under the blanket that covered her; Tina, four months pregnant, stroking Mom's lifeless feet through peach-colored anklets.

I sat down on a chair beside the couch, but I couldn't look at my mother. I stared straight ahead and tried to keep a lid on my emotions, especially my anger. Why was she still here with all these people swarming around her body?

Several minutes passed, and a voice somewhere in my head kept telling me I had to look at my mother. She had said often that she did not want the coffin open at her funeral, did not want people gathering around and staring down at her. This would be the last time I would see her.

The voice nagged at me until I turned to face her. I was relieved that I couldn't see her face, only the back of her head and a portion of her right cheek. I leaned forward and touched her. Even through the blanket I could feel the bones of her arm and shoulder.

God, she is so fragile, I thought. In an instant, the anger returned. She was dead, dead for hours, maybe, with people milling around like they were backstage at the Opry.

Martha Dettwiller, one of Mom's and my best friends, called while I was in that state of mind. She had driven to the house a little earlier, but Doug Anderson had turned her away.

"Why is she still here, Martha?" I asked, hoping she could explain this maddening scene to me. I hadn't had much experience with these matters, but I was pretty sure it was not normal for a deceased person to be lying around for hours before a doctor or ambulance or funeral home was called. When my grandmother died several years ago, I remembered, the coroner was called and he came to the house to officially pronounce her dead. The funeral home removed her immediately. It was nothing like this.

"This is not right," I told Martha. "Why is she here?"

"Honey, I don't know," she said.

Only one person knew and it seemed pointless to ask him.

Richey was sobbing and babbling and appeared to be near collapse. The most lucid he had been all evening was shortly after Tina arrived. He was sitting in the hall, in a chair by the fish tank, and as Tina walked past, he said, "I don't want her to be autopsied. She's been cut on too many times."

Most of the night, he stayed in his office or made a

quick trip to the kitchen, literally held up by one of his brothers.

About all I could learn from Gwen was that she had received a call at seven-thirty and had called Tina and me immediately.

Gwen lived just a short distance from Mom, so she was at the house five minutes after receiving the call. The first person she saw when she got there was a lawyer friend of Richey's. Gwen was upset, but not so much that that oddity slipped past her.

Why was a lawyer called before the children of the deceased were notified?

Most of Richey's family was already there, too, having been notified before any of Mom's daughters.

My youngest sister, Georgette, who is a nurse in Alexander City, Alabama, was not notified at all. Mom's housekeeper had called Gwen and left it up to her to call her three sisters. Unaware that Georgette was on duty at the hospital that night, Gwen left a message on her home phone that Georgette never received. Georgette called the house just after ten and told us she had learned of Mom's death from a coworker who had heard about it on TV.

It was slowly becoming apparent that Tammy Wynette's daughters were the last to learn of her passing.

Gwen didn't dwell on that, though, not immediately. At the time, she was more troubled by the scene at the house. It was even more chaotic than when I arrived two hours later. So many people were milling around Mom's body that Gwen asked Doug to clear the room. Then she placed chairs across the doorways to discourage traffic through the room. She asked Doug not to let anyone but family members into the house after that.

She was becoming angry and it occurred to her that if a lawyer had already been summoned, surely a doctor had been called, too. She asked Sylvia about it and was told that no local doctor had been notified.

"Nobody will come out because she doesn't have a doctor here," Sylvia told her.

"That's a crock of shit," Gwen snapped. "Davidson County has a medical examiner. He will come out."

"Well," Sylvia said, "Dr. Marsh is on his way from Pittsburgh."

Dr. Wallis Marsh was a respected liver-transplant specialist at the University of Pittsburgh Medical Center. He had been treating Mom for a variety of ailments for about six years. He'd become more than her doctor: he was a friend and fan who sometimes went on cruises or performance tours, almost like a part of Mom's entourage.

As far as we knew, he was an excellent physician and surgeon, but it made no sense to me or my sisters why he would charter a plane and fly all the way from Pittsburgh just to sign her death certificate. Nashville was full of doctors capable of doing that. Davidson County had a medical examiner who could have done that. Why send for a doctor nearly six hundred miles away?

Before Gwen could pursue the issue, Tina, who was standing near a walk-in closet, caught her eye.

"Gwen, come here," she said.

Gwen walked over and saw a household worker removing items from Mom's purse and elsewhere in the closet— items that appeared to include Mom's medications.

When I walked into the house, I was a knot of shock, confusion and anger. I couldn't think clearly. Everything felt wrong but I didn't know why. Frankly, in the commotion I didn't know what questions to ask, and even if I did,

I don't think anyone in that house could, or would, have answered them.

Of course, the cause of my mother's death was an obvious question, but about all that Gwen and Tina and I could learn, or surmise, was that Richey had found her dead and called his lawyer, his own family members, and a doctor almost six hundred miles away—in which order I didn't know. Why this strange scenario?

That was the first of many troubling questions surrounding Mom's death, but that night I was too weary and too dazed to articulate them—even to myself. The scene at the house went from surreal to macabre to infuriating. Maybe sanity would prevail the next day, but for the moment, I just wanted to get out of there. I didn't want to be there when they took Mom away. I couldn't bear to watch them put her in a bag and wheel her out of her home.

"I'm ready to go," I told Larry.

We walked down the hall, past Richey's office, and into the cool spring air. The last thing we heard before the door closed behind us was Richey's interminable wail, "She's gone . . . she's gone . . . my baby's gone."

EARLY TUESDAY MORNING, Nanette Crafton, Mom's friend and former hairdresser, came by and picked up my girls and took them to school. She offered to keep them the entire week so I would be free to attend to Mom's funeral and other details that would fall to us.

I called my boss at EuroTan and told him I was taking the week off, which didn't surprise him because the news of Mom's death had dominated the radio and television newscasts for the past twelve hours. Nashville is a large city and country music is not the dominant cog in its economy. Despite its size, the music community is only the stitching of the city's cultural and social fabric. When one of its stars gets married, divorced, busted, or dies, the airwaves and grapevines start to crackle.

Larry had a nine o'clock flight to Florida, so I dropped him at the airport and drove to Martha Dettwiller's house. I needed to see a friendly face, someone I could talk to. The minute I saw Martha, all my tensions just broke free and I began crying and nearly slumped into her lap. Neither of us could believe Mom really was gone.

"I just saw her yesterday," I said.

"I know, honey," she said, putting her arm around me and trying to comfort me as best she could.

I told her about the bizarre scene the night before. "Martha, we don't even know what she died from," I said. "I left at eleven and no doctor had been to the house. Marsh was on his way from Pittsburgh. I don't know if he got here or if he's still around."

"Don't worry," she said. "Everything will fall into place. Everything will work out."

Martha was not upset at being turned away from the house the night before. Doug had explained to her that only family was being admitted. My anger had not been focused on anyone in particular but on the outrageous scenario I had walked into. Maybe Richey had been too shocked to know what to do. Maybe no one else in the house knew how to handle the situation, or wanted to handle it without Richey's permission.

Martha and I must have talked and cried for more than two hours while she prepared some food to take to Mom's house. Gradually we both began to feel a little better.

What we didn't know was that Marsh had arrived sometime after midnight, signed a death certificate and released

Mom's body to the Woodlawn Funeral Home. We did not know that as we sat there, consoling each other, she had already been embalmed and that the blood that had been drained from her veins and organs carried with it truths we would never know, secrets we would never penetrate.

Two

IT WAS MID-AFTERNOON before I left Martha's and drove to Mom's house. Georgette had gotten to Nashville in the wee hours, so all my sisters were there, along with a houseful of other people—relatives, friends and fans.

Wallis Marsh was there, too. After filling out the death certificate, he had spent the night at the house and was in the kitchen when I approached him.

"Dr. Marsh, what happened?" I asked.

He was as somber as everyone else on the premises. "She had a blood clot to the lungs, an embolism," he said. "All her counts had been good. Her weight was good. Everything was good. . . ."

I wasn't sure when Marsh had seen her last, but Mom had a home health-care nurse who came regularly, so he must have been relying on information provided by her for that analysis.

At the time I had no basis for doubting his opinion. Because of Mom's frequent hospital stays and surgeries over the years, I had become familiar with some medical terminology, but I certainly lacked the knowledge to question the conclusion of such a distinguished authority as Dr. Marsh.

But I did not agree that her "weight was good" and I doubted that her "counts" were, either. Although she had her good days, she had become so weak that performing had been almost impossible for her for the past few months. Was he trying to tell me she was in reasonably good health and this blood clot appeared from nowhere?

"Well, why did she die?" I asked.

There was a short pause before he said, "Well, she died . . . peacefully. She died in her sleep. She was in no pain."

That told me how she died, but not why.

I thanked him and went to find my sisters. I assumed we had a funeral to plan. I was wrong.

Richey seemed to have bounced back from his crippling bereavement of the previous night. He stayed mostly in his office with his brother Paul, who, along with Frank Mull, Richey's longtime friend, was planning the funeral and public memorial. "Brother, did you call Randy Travis?" we could hear him say. "What about Wynonna?" He was fully in control.

Later, though, when Martha came by with a ham and potato salad, he apparently was in no shape to invite her into the house. The housekeeper was taking the food when George and Nancy Jones arrived. Richey suddenly appeared outside his office. He made brief eye contact with Martha and again broke into howling sobs. Someone had to lead him away.

Martha thought he was just too emotional to talk to her. She asked the housekeeper if she needed anything else and went to the grocery store with a list the housekeeper gave her. When she got back, she wasn't even invited into the foyer. The housekeeper took the bags at the door and thanked her.

While Richey was being lucid in private and sobbing incoherently in the presence of visitors, his brother continued to plan the funeral and the big show at the Ryman. All I knew was that Tammy Wynette's daughters would have little say or much to do in either, except to go to the Woodlawn Funeral Home and select a casket and the crypt at the mausoleum.

We were preparing to leave about the time George and Nancy arrived.

Jones had been Mom's third husband, and during their stormy six years together, they had been the toast, and sometimes the scandal, of Nashville. They were known affectionately as the President and First Lady of Country Music, but Jones's drunken, violent binges finally drove them apart. They continued to perform together occasionally and were good friends, which pleased me. I truly loved Jones. He was as kind and gentle and generous as anyone I have ever known, and he had an endearing sense of humor and humility. I have always believed that he was the one man Mom married for the right reason: love. I also believe she carried a torch for him to her grave. She had become infatuated with him when he was nothing more than a voice on the radio wave beamed out to her boondocks, and in spite of the turbulence of their marriage and messy breakup, I never heard her say an unkind word about him except occasionally in jest. She spent most of her life holding one firm belief: that George Jones was the greatest country singer who ever lived, and in her mind that offset many of his personal failings.

When he and Nancy came into the house that day, I saw Jones embrace Hazel Hall, my grandmother's first cousin. She and her husband, Dan, had driven up from Red Bay, Alabama, to attend the funeral.

"Hazel, we've lost a good friend," Jones said.

He was wiping tears from his eyes. Until that day, I had never seen him cry.

When I told him we were going to pick out a casket, he and Nancy insisted on coming along to help in any way they could. Their presence was a real comfort to me and to Georgette. She was the only offspring of Jones and Mom's union, but she had never been particularly close to her dad, probably because her childhood coincided with the worst of his drinking years. But he had changed and Georgette had grown up; their relationship was really just beginning to strengthen and grow.

At the funeral parlor, we went into a family room to visit with the funeral director for a few minutes before being escorted into a large room that reminded me of a car dealer's showroom. There were rows and stacks of polished wood and metal caskets in every imaginable color, each upholstered with fine white fabrics. I've never understood why so much effort and expense goes into something that is seen so fleetingly before it's sealed in a vault or covered with dirt.

Jones and Nancy stayed with us the entire time. It took only a few minutes to select the coffin, but there was another matter to be handled that day, something the morticians would normally handle.

"I want to do it," Georgette said, when the subject of dressing Mom for burial came up. "I don't want strange people staring at her."

I admired my sister's grit. Even if I had wanted to participate, I could not have brought myself to do it. But Georgette and Gwen and Deirdre, Richey's daughter, were up to the task. They dressed Mom in a simple cream-colored pleated skirt and matching jacket. Two of her friends, Wanda Burgess and Liz Linneman, did her hair and makeup.

Neither I nor any of my sisters was consulted about the funeral service. I was told that there would be no visitation prior to the funeral, only the private service and the public memorial afterward. Richey and his brother Paul made all the decisions regarding both. The public affair was by far the most demanding. Paul and Frank Mull were assembling a lineup of celebrities, all of whom had been close to Mom, to fill a two-hour show, which Paul would produce and direct.

We were never asked about a format for the funeral service or who we wanted to include in the memorial—or if we wanted the memorial at all. Yes, my mother had many friends and legions of fans who would want to say good-bye to her in some way, but this way made me uneasy. Mom was very private in her own way, and I couldn't convince myself that this was what she would want, at least not on the day of her burial. It would have thrilled her to know that her friends had gathered to sing songs to her and share memories of her with each other, but on worldwide television? I had doubts.

After we returned to the house from the funeral home on Tuesday afternoon, I discovered I was not the only one of my siblings harboring them.

Tina had been on edge from the very beginning, but I had interpreted that as just her nature. She had always been wound a little tighter than the rest of us, was more rebellious and impulsive. She was a talented singer—she and

Georgette sang backup for Mom one summer—and Mom had hopes of her finding a place in the business, but I don't think Tina really wanted that. She was independent and restless and followed her own mind.

"Something's not right," Tina said that night, when the four of us finally had a few minutes to talk.

"What do you mean?" I asked her. She had put into words what I had been feeling for twenty-four hours but was afraid to even think about. I had been flowing through the ordeal along the path of least resistance, taking everything at face value.

"I mean that something's just not right."

Georgette, who had some training and experience in medical matters, was more precise in her suspicions.

"I don't know how Marsh could be sure it was a blood clot that killed her," she said. "You can't tell that without an autopsy."

I didn't pursue it with her any further. A couple of old friends were arriving from out of town and staying at my apartment, so I left to meet them. In a way it was heartening to learn that I was not the only one carrying around a vague uneasiness, though it was hardly comforting to know the consensus was that something seemed wrong.

JAN SMITH IS Nanette Crafton's sister. She is also a hairdresser who worked for Mom off and on for years and during Mom's marriage to Jones. After Mom married Richey in 1978, Jan decided to get off the road and turned most of her duties over to Nan. Both sisters were like family.

Mom didn't have employees, she had friends, and if they happened to be on her payroll, fine, but they were friends first. Maybe because Mom had been a beauty operator before she became a singer, she felt a certain kinship with her hairdressers; they were like sisters to her. She shopped with them, went to lunch with them, and sometimes they sat up together until dawn, gossiping and giggling like schoolgirls.

Jan and Mom met in the late 1960s, when Mom was still kind of new to the business and nobody knew her very well. She went to the Nashville Municipal Auditorium one rainy night to be in a show with several other acts, including June Carter and Johnny Cash. Jan, who fixed June's hair, was backstage when Mom walked in, soaked and looking a little lost.

Jan went over to her and said, "Aren't you Tammy Wynette?"

"Yes," Mom said.

"You look like a drowned rat," said Jan, who's inclined to speak her mind. "Let's go do something with you before you go on stage."

Not long after that, Jan became a fixture in Mom's entourage and continued to work for her off and on until well into the 1980s.

Along with other friends of Mom's, she was at the house on Wednesday when I went by.

I could tell immediately that something was bothering her. All of the press reports had stated that Richey had found his wife dead at seven o'clock on Monday night, and I had not talked to anybody who questioned that. Until I talked to Jan.

"Jackie," she asked, "did the doctor tell you what time Tammy died?"

"No . . . I guess not. All I know is that Richey found her at seven."

"I want to tell you something weird," Jan said. "I had a

call from a friend at five-thirty Monday afternoon. He said, 'Jan, I don't want you to hear this on the news, but a good friend just called and told me Tammy is dead.' "

For a minute, I felt like my circuits had shorted out. I couldn't quite absorb what she was telling me.

"Five-thirty . . . ? How is that possible? Are you sure?"

"Yes. I kept watching the television thinking there would be a news report. I called your mother's house several times, but the line was always busy. Finally, there was a news bulletin on TV . . . sometime before ten."

Either Jan was confused about the time, which I doubted, or Richey wasn't telling the whole story about the time that he found Mom. But why? And if she did die earlier, how did Jan's friend hear about it so quickly? Why wasn't I or any of my sisters contacted sooner? I had no answers and neither did Jan, but I was becoming convinced that there was more to my mother's death than I'd originally suspected. What, I didn't know, but I was determined to find out.

Mark Crawford, my mother's groundskeeper, was always around during the day, so I found him and asked him about Monday. Sure enough, he had arrived at the house by eight o'clock that morning.

"Did you see Mom?" I asked him.

"Yeah, I saw her early that morning. She was on that couch where she died."

"Was she sitting up?"

"No, she was lying down when I got here," he said. "That's where she was when I came by."

"I know," he said. "I left at five-thirty and she was in the same position . . . hadn't moved all day."

"How could she sleep that long?" I asked, more or less rhetorically. Mark had a funny look on his face.

"Jackie, you know how your mom made that little grunting sound when she was sleeping?" he said. Of course I knew. Everyone who lived or traveled with Mom for the last several years knew. It wasn't exactly a snore, but something between a murmur and a groan, the fitful sound of someone dead to the world.

"Yeah . . ."

"Well, she wasn't sleeping like that. She wasn't making that noise."

A shiver went down my back as I realized that I hadn't heard her trademark grunting when I was there either.

Was it possible that she had been dead all day? Why did Richey not notice until seven o'clock? Or why did he say he did not find her dead until seven? Why couldn't a renowned doctor like Wallis Marsh determine more accurately the time of death? If he had made such a determination, if he knew she had died much earlier, why didn't he discuss that with my sisters and me? We not only didn't know why she died, we didn't know when.

Richey had been in charge of Mom's household and her business for years. Dr. Marsh had been in charge of her health care for years. But they were volunteering nothing.

THAT NIGHT, MOM'S casket was placed in a visitation room at the funeral home. Earlier, we had agreed that there would be no wake, except for the immediate family. But when we arrived at the funeral home, there was a crowd of entertainers, their families, and other music-industry people mingling around her open coffin.

I guess it's customary for a casket to be open during wakes, but I wish Mom's had not been. She would not have wanted that either. She never wanted people looking down at her in a box and here we all were, gazing down at someone who didn't even look like my mother. Her face was twice its normal size and it seemed that she had no neck. Her lips were broad and stretched.

She would not have wanted people to see her that way, and my sisters and I thought we had made the decision to prevent that from happening. But our wishes had been overruled.

Seeing her like that made my heart ache. Blood rushed to my head. I wanted to ask someone, "Why does she look like that?" But this wasn't the time or place. Instead, the question went into my mental file of unanswered questions, a file that was thickening almost by the hour.

Three

My MEMORY OF the funeral service at Judson Baptist Church is largely a blur of colors and sounds: Mom's closed casket and an altar laden with huge wreaths and sprays and potted greenery, organ music and hymns and prayers and eulogies, hugs and handshakes and many tearful faces I had not seen in a long time.

Mom had not attended church regularly in many years, so there was no natural choice of a pastor to officiate at her funeral. Richey asked a friend of his, Dr. James Murray, to preside. I read later that he delivered a "moving eulogy," but I don't really recall what he said. It had been a disturbing week and I had not slept well. Given all the clamor and confusion, and my lack of sleep, my powers of concentration were seriously diminished.

In some ways, I guess, I also felt like an intruder at my mother's funeral. Nearly all of the arrangements had been made by her husband and his family. That feeling of being forced out seemed like one more unpleasant reality I had no choice but to accept.

Later, I would learn that other people very dear to Mom were not treated particularly well either.

HAZEL HALL, A first cousin to my grandmother Mildred, helped raise my mother. Mom enjoyed her companionship and probably confided in her as much as anyone. I know that over the years, whenever Mom got homesick or restless, she would call Hazel and say, "I've got to put in my order," meaning she was on her way to Red Bay, Alabama, and wanted Hazel to cook something special for her.

A few years ago, there was a hard snowstorm blowing across the South and I guess Mom was feeling caged up and lonesome. She called Hazel and said, "I want you to come to Nashville."

"Now look," Hazel argued, "me and Dan are not as young as you are. We're not going to start out in a car on these slick roads."

"You've got to come," Mom insisted.

"You know we can't drive up there in this snow."

Mom was obviously disappointed and Hazel thought that was the last of it. An hour later, her phone rang again.

"Would you come if I sent my bus down to pick you up?" Mom asked her.

"You're not going to send that big bus down here just for me and Dan," Hazel said, thinking Mom was joking.

"I am, too," Mom said. "At eight o'clock tomorrow morning, it will be sitting in your driveway."

I doubt that there was anyone in Mom's family who meant more to her than Hazel and Dan Hall. Naturally, they came to Nashville immediately when she died, but when they walked into the church that Thursday, they learned they would be seated at the back of the chapel, not with the family near the altar.

Hazel was offended by the slight. She and Dan had planned to attend the public memorial at the Ryman later that day, but after the funeral, she told her husband, "We're going home."

ON THE MORNING of the funeral, Martha Dettwiller went to the office of Evelyn Shriver, who had been Mom's publicist for many years, and volunteered to help out with the sudden workload. All week, Evelyn's phone had rung constantly. Reporters from all over the world were hounding her for more information about Mom's death, wanting her to confirm or deny the latest rumor.

That morning, Evelyn asked her to call Mom's house and request passes for relatives and friends at the Ryman memorial.

Sylvia answered the phone and sounded very testy.

"Did Evelyn tell you to do this?" Sylvia asked.

Martha exhaled sharply and said, "Sylvia, I'm at Evelyn's office. She asked me to call you and she wants me to come by and pick up the passes. Do you have some there at the house?"

"Yes," Sylvia said. Martha detected a haughtiness that puzzled her.

"Well, I will come by before the funeral and pick them up."

When she got to the house, Martha was told that the passes were not there, that someone had taken them to the church. At Judson Baptist, Martha parked her car and saw

Lorrie Morgan standing by the back door. She decided to go in that way, rather than through the front, which was fortunate because she might not have gotten in otherwise. She found a seat in the chapel next to Mike Martinovich and left her purse there while she came to a small room where the family had gathered to wait to be seated. We talked for a few minutes, and then Martha started back to the chapel.

In the vestibule, Sylvia stepped in front of her and said, "You can't go in this way."

Martha pointed at a pew just inside the doorway where Mike was sitting.

"My seat is right there. My purse is right there. I will go in this way," she said, pushing her way past Sylvia.

Martha told me later that someone at the church had informed her that the word was spread that she was not to be allowed into the church.

OUTSIDE THE RYMAN, television cameras weaved and bobbed among the crowd that had been waiting in line for hours to get inside. Anyone who stood still for a few minutes was subject to being interviewed. I had been on tour with Mom, but I guess that in my mind her fans were just shadowy faces in a darkened theater. Now they were real people, thousands of them, vivid and sunlit, huddled in parkas and scarves against the cold wind.

I saw a reporter with a microphone close to his mouth, his voice being transmitted through satellites to distant places I could only imagine.

Tammy Wynette is being remembered here at the Ryman Auditorium, which is appropriate because

*from 1943 to 1974 the Ryman was the home of the
Grand Ole Opry. Many people considered Tammy to
be the First Lady of Country. Two thousand seats in
this auditorium, each one of them is filled. The family
of Tammy Wynette wanted this to be a public service.
There was a private memorial held earlier today attended by a number of her peers and family and
friends. This one they wanted to be public. . . .*

Who wanted it to be public? Tammy Wynette's daughters were never asked, and if we had been, we probably
would have said no. But, after the decision was made to
hold a public memorial, there was another battle to be
fought. Evelyn wanted Mom's body taken to the Ryman
for that service, and, apparently, so did Richey.

Deirdre asked Gwen and Georgette if that was what
they wanted and they said, "No." She agreed with them,
but Paul Richardson persisted. "Her fans would like to see
her casket there," he kept saying.

Since our desires hadn't carried much weight, I didn't
know what to expect when we got to the Ryman. It would
not have surprised me to see Mom's casket center stage.

Fortunately it was not, but even without her being there,
I was overwhelmed with emotion as soon as I walked into
the auditorium. The stage bore a luminous mound of flowers. In the foreground were two huge portraits of Mom—
beauty-queen portraits, the way she looked before her
body was ravaged by drugs and surgeons' scalpels.

At the end of her time, she had shriveled to under 100
pounds and looked much older than her fifty-five years. In
my head, those framed images collided with the memories
of the night she died, when she was frail and drawn and

brittle, and with the memories of the way she looked in the open coffin.

Tears streamed down my face as we took our seats.

Dr. Murray gave an opening prayer and J. D. Summer & the Stamps sang "Peace in the Valley," and then Randy Travis came on to sing "Precious Memories." God bless Randy. He came all the way from Mexico to be there, which didn't surprise me. For five years, he had been the opening act for Mom's show. After he became a star and had his own act, they sometimes performed on the same bill. Mom was also fond of his wife, Lib. They shared a passion for country cooking. Once, Randy was touring Europe and Mom was getting ready to hook up with him there. Lib called her before she left and asked her to bring a couple of items with her: fatback and beans. Mom did, and they commandeered a hotel kitchen to cook for everyone.

Naomi Judd followed Randy on stage, and was herself followed by her daughter, Wynonna. Lorrie Morgan and Dolly Parton were there, as were the Oak Ridge Boys and Rudy Gatlin. These were busy people, yet they managed, on two or three days' notice, to fit this day into their schedules. They will always have a special place in my heart for making that effort.

Still, the public memorial made me uneasy. *Mom would not have wanted this,* I kept thinking. It was too much like . . . what? . . . another show. Too much production and staging and lighting effects. But I have to be honest: When Dolly Parton sang "I Will Always Love You," I nearly lost it. The raw, exquisite emotional power of that moment took my breath away.

After Lorrie Morgan sang "Amazing Grace," she looked toward our family and said, "I have a few words I want to add to this wonderful tribute to my idol, Tammy Wynette. To her children, I'm sorry. To her husband, I'm sorry. To her friends, I'm sorry. And I heard Naomi talking a little while ago about—that [Tammy's] children are what kept her going on the road. And that's the same way that it is with me. My children inspire me and keep me going on the road. But also a very important part of my life that keeps me going on the road is my band . . ."

She waved her arm in the direction of the musicians behind her.

" . . . and Tammy's band . . . Young Country."

The audience rose in ovation. As the applause continued, Richey appeared on stage, escorted—almost held up—by his son and daughter. He made his way to Lorrie and embraced her and buried his face in her shoulder.

She patted him and said, "I love you, George. I'm going to sing you a song. Okay? Do you want to stand up here when we do this?"

Richey said, "Uh-huh" but never lifted his head from her shoulder.

"Do you want to say something?" she asked him.

"Yes," he said, reaching for the microphone with his head bowed and his body leaning as though he might topple forward.

"Take a deep breath," Lorrie said, holding on to him.

I glanced at Gwen and recognized my own feelings etched in her face. Richey's voice sounded to us like the pathetic whimper of an abused puppy. There was teardrop and tragedy in his every syllable.

"I guess I would have to thank Billy Sherrill for finding her," he moaned, "because if he hadn't found her, I'm sure I wouldn't have found her. I love you, Billy. She loved you."

His head was still down, his shoulders hunched and his hands clasped as if in prayer around the microphone. With a white handkerchief he wiped his right eye and then his nose.

"For a long time . . . a few years . . . maybe four or five, I was never away from her for more than thirty minutes . . . maybe . . . because that's what I wanted . . . was to look after her. She was my buddy. And I didn't think it would happen the way it did, but we were alone in the house on the couch when she left, just me and her."

His words were hoarse and halting and the pain excruciatingly pronounced.

"Oh, my God," he quavered. "Oooohhh. Oooohhh. Billy, thank you. Jones, thank you. Nancy, thank you. All my kids and the grandkids, I love you."

Georgette looked at me, and I mouthed the words, *Get him off that stage,* knowing full well that she was as powerless as I to do that.

Before he could go on, Lorrie took the microphone from his hand and his two escorts took him by the arms and led him off stage. Backed by Mom's band, Lorrie then sang "Stand by Your Man" and the service was over.

Most of Mom's friends gathered on the stage as the portraits and flowers were removed. Many of the spectators stood and watched in silence for a long time.

On the drive home, I told Nanette Crafton, "You know what that public memorial was all about. It was the George Richey Show."

She said nothing. It would be a while before many of Mom's friends would open their hearts and tell me what they really knew and thought about the last years of her life.

PART TWO

Neon Rainbows

Four

EVERY TIME I look at the pictures of that old house, it is hard to believe that it was my first home, that I was born there. It was an old, listing shanty—built in the nineteenth century and allowed to slowly deteriorate ever since—in the woods behind the farm in Itawamba County, Mississippi, where my great-grandparents Chester and Flora Russell lived.

There were no indoor toilets or running water, and I remember Mom talking about how she cooked in the fireplace and washed clothes outside in a cauldron over an open fire. The house had a creaky tin roof, plank floors, and cracks in the walls, which Mom and Dad patched with pieces of cardboard.

Mom had to carry water from a spring on the farm. She couldn't take Gwen or me with her, and it wasn't safe to leave us alone for the time it would take to make the two-hundred-yard round trip, so she found a way to anchor us while she was gone. I was still young enough to be imprisoned in my baby bed, but to keep Gwen from crawling away or getting into trouble, she would lift up the bedpost and set it down on the hem of Gwen's dress.

Naturally, I don't have many direct memories of those days—just the stories I have heard and the photographs I have seen. For a long time, my impression was that my mother had been born into poverty and so had Gwen and Tina and I.

It wasn't until I was older that a relative told me, "Chester had money. He just didn't spend it."

Grandpa Russell was hardworking, industrious, entre-preneurial and as frugal as a pawnbroker. By the time he was in his twenties, he owned a sawmill and was saving for the six hundred acres of farmland he would soon buy. Like many small farmers, who live and die by the whims of the seasons, he valued security above comfort, or at least above luxury. Next year's crop was always a gamble, but money in the bank was the featherbed of a good night's sleep.

When I think back on my mother's life, that farm and the sensibilities it fashioned in her lie at the core of who and what she was. From that land, I believe, came the seeds of all that was shining and all that was tragic in her.

Her love of cooking came from that place, from a grand-mother who made fresh biscuits every morning and whose kitchen always smelled of a ham baking in the oven and collard greens and pinto beans—the comfort foods of the South—stewing in black iron pots on the stovetop. Mom watched and learned, but sometimes, as she did throughout her life, she insisted on swimming outside the buoys.

When she was nine or ten years old, she decided to sur-prise everyone by making cornbread for dinner. No one was around that afternoon, or no one was paying any attention to her, so she slipped into the kitchen, got a big bowl from the cabinet and started mixing up eggs and flour and milk and cornmeal.

Thinking she would fancy it up a bit, she splashed in a generous dose of green cake coloring. The cornbread tasted fine, Mom always laughed, but everyone in the family was afraid to eat it.

Her love of music also came from that place.

Her father's name was William Hollice Pugh, and he died when she was nine months old. His family, too, had been farmers; but he had an extraordinary musical talent, and when he and my grandmother Mildred were married, he often talked about his dream of becoming a professional musician. He had no formal training but could play just about any instrument he set his mind to.

Married only a year and with a child on the way, he found out that he would never realize that dream, or any other. He was diagnosed with a brain tumor and given only a few months to live, but he survived long enough to see his child and introduce her to music.

The baby girl was christened Virginia Wynette Pugh, and her father spent as much time as he could with her, even as the tumor began to rob him of his eyesight.

One of their favorite activities involved the piano. He would sit for hours with Mom on his lap, placing her hands on the keys and picking out a song. He could not possibly have recognized musical talent in a six- or seven-month-old baby, but there was no mistaking her fascination with the keys and the sounds that flowed in response to her touch.

"Mildred, I want you to promise me something," he would tell my grandmother. "I want you to promise that you'll see to it that this child is taught music."

It was a promise Mildred didn't have to keep. With no help from her, or from anyone else, little Virginia Wynette seemed compelled by the genes passed down from her father.

Hollice Pugh died on February 13, 1943, and Mildred, facing bleak employment prospects close to home, went to Memphis to work in a defense plant. She left her daughter in the care of her parents, Chester and Flora Russell, and others in the extended family who were willing to care for her.

One of those was Hazel Hall, Mildred's first cousin, who had a daughter, Jane, about Mom's age. From when she was less than a year old, Mom spent a lot of time at Hazel's house, where one of her favorite pastimes was tinkering with the piano. By the time she was four or five—still too small to climb onto the bench—she stood in front of the keys and, with no instruction, picked simple melodies.

When they were old enough, Hazel signed Mom and Jane up for weekly piano lessons from a local teacher. Between lessons, Jane practiced the drills the teacher had given them, but Mom rarely did. Instead, she played the music she wanted to play.

One day the teacher called Hazel and said, "You tell Nette's mother that it's important that I see her and talk to her."

"Is it something bad?" Hazel asked.

"No, but it's important," he said.

When Mildred came home for a visit, she went to see the teacher.

"You're wasting your money," he told her.

Mildred was crushed. "You mean she's not learning it?" she said.

"No, I mean I can play a song one time and she can repeat it," he said. "It's got me mind-boggled. This girl doesn't need lessons. She just needs a piano."

Later, Mildred asked her, "Honey, do you practice?"

Mom said, "No, I just play. If I hear a song, I know how to play it."

ONE OF MOM'S closest childhood friends was Linda Cayson, who was also her first partner in performing professionally. Actually, you couldn't call it professional, since they weren't paid, but even before they were teenagers they were regulars on the local church and small-town radio circuit. Linda sang melody and Mom sang harmony and, for the most part, they stuck to the gospel standards that gave rhythm to the hellfire and brimstone of the fundamentalist sanctuaries of the South. How many country singers trace their musical roots to small church choirs? An easier question is, how many don't?

Mom and Linda became popular enough that by the time they were thirteen or fourteen they were invited to sing on a live television broadcast out of Tupelo, Mississippi, the birthplace of Elvis Presley. They wouldn't be limited to church tunes, either. It was a chance to rock 'n' roll.

It was the mid-1950s and television was still new. Local stations especially depended on live programming, so there were no second takes. If you screwed up, it was on the airwaves for all the world—well, all the county—to see. Some of those small stations broadcast with barely enough power to reach the city limits.

But it was the biggest thing that had happened to Mom and Linda, and they went all out for it. They got new hair-

dos and bought identical, frilly little dresses with V necks
that gave just a tease of the cleavage that might one day
exist.

They took their place in front of the camera with the
bright studio lights beating down on them like heat lamps.
They ignored the perspiration forming on their skin and
jumped right into an Everly Brothers song.

Out of nowhere, a huge, flying insect flitted in front of
the lights, made a lap around the studio and landed on
Linda's chest, nestling itself between her breasts.

Without missing a beat or veering off-key, Linda
reached inside her dress, found the bug and removed it.

They were too thrilled about being on television to be
embarrassed by the incident.

Linda and Mom started first grade together in a school
so small it only had three or four teachers. Until Mom got
married, just before they were to graduate from high
school, she and Linda were almost inseparable. It was a
friendship that became a template for other bonds that
Mom formed in later years. She and Linda shared everything, confided in each other, defended each other, played
pranks on each other and leaned on each other for support.

Memories and insights that Linda has shared with me
are poignant and revealing, so I will share them with you,
in her words:

> In high school, I got into a big ruckus with an-
> other girl. She was older and quite a bit bigger than
> me, and I thought she was going to beat me up. As
> small as she was, Tammy came to my rescue. She got
> right up in the other girl's face and wanted to really
> tell her off, but she couldn't cuss. In those days, that
> was just something girls didn't do. But she wanted to

say something bad, so she blurted out, "You're just a blamed ol' Communist." I guess in the fifties, calling someone a Communist was as bad as anything short of profanity, but it had a hilarious ring to it.

She was always funny. One time we went up to Birmingham to visit one of her uncles and his family. She fixed me up with her cousin and he fixed her up with one of his friends. We went to a big park and just walked around all afternoon, and we ended up sitting on a bench. The boys were back to back and Tammy and I were facing them, so we could see each other. We were kissing these boys, and I opened my eyes and she had her eyes wide open and was making faces at me while she was kissing her date. We both cracked up and that kind of ended it. The boys thought we were laughing at them. They didn't go out with us again.

Tammy liked boys from an early age, and that sometimes made trouble for me. When we were in the ninth grade, we were dating two brothers—sons of a preacher—and Tammy got the idea she was going to elope and I was going to have to be her cover, her accomplice. Well, the plot didn't go very far before Mildred got wind of it and put a stop to it, but we were both in the dog house for a couple of weeks.

Boys, and later men, were always complicating her life. It seems kind of strange now, but I remember one summer when we picked cotton together and all Tammy talked about was this new country singer named George Jones. She thought he was the grandest thing.

When she first left town to try a singing career, she wanted me to go with her and sing backup, but I was from the old school and wouldn't think about leaving home. Even after she got real big, I would visit her in Nashville and we would get in the car and go for a drive and she'd say, "Lin, let's see if we can still do it." We'd drive around for the longest time singing "Amazing Grace," "Swing Low, Sweet Chariot," "How Great Thou Art" and all the old gospel songs that we had performed when we were kids.

Toward me and, I'm sure, everyone else from back home, she never changed when she became a big star and was making tons of money. I would go to her home, and I'd be in bed and I would hear a tapping on the door. She would come in wearing her old nightgown and she'd plop down on the bed, and it would be just like it was years and years ago. We would talk until the wee hours. A lot of bad things happened to her over the years, but she was still the liveliest, funniest person I knew. Right up to the end, she could tickle you to death.

But I often felt sad for her, too. She spent her whole life looking for happiness, but she never really found it, never found what she should have had. I know she felt a deep love for the people in country music . . . they were like family. And she loved to perform, to entertain. But there came a time when I believed that the business was destroying her. Her career had peaked and tapered off, but she kept pushing herself, even when she was too sick to go on stage. I asked her why she didn't just give it up.

She said, "There's just something . . . once you have a number-one hit, you're always searching for the next one."

Stories such as those help me to understand my mother in subtle ways. She had dreamed young and dreamed hard, and she achieved everything she could envision—except happiness. Success for her was not a placid lake but a churning river of erratic and conflicting currents.

Her own internal contradictions were heightened by the two worlds that tugged at her. Growing up around places like Tremont, Mississippi, and Red Bay, Alabama, had instilled in her a love of family and community—the very treasures she'd have to renounce for the sake of wanderlust and ambition.

She always loved going back home, but I think she was forever driven by a horror of *having* to go back home, to a place that was anathema to her nature.

She was daring and adventurous, but "back home" was an authoritarian mother who told her whom she could and couldn't date. She was fiercely independent and self-reliant, but "back home" included the only period in her life when she had been dependent on a man. She was hooked on the highway and the spotlight, but "back home" was a place of quiet streets that folded up at sundown.

Sometimes when Mom talked about her failed marriages, she would admit that she got into unhappy relationships because she could not stand to be alone. She needed a man, a companion, a lover, someone to share her life, but the life she lived was a hard one to share. I don't know how any marriage can survive the demands of 250 days a year on the road. Mom never left any doubt about her priorities.

"I would never give up the road for a husband," she would tell anyone who asked.

And yes, the same sentiment applied to her daughters.

Five

"THE WAY I see it, my mother had a goal—she wanted to be an entertainer and her family was secondary. She was gone all the time."

I blurted out those words to Jane Sanderson of *People* magazine without giving much thought as to how harsh they sounded. It was something I'd felt but had repressed for years. Sure, Mom knew how I felt—how all of her daughters felt—but I had never given those feelings a public voice. It was probably because the journalists who swarmed around my mother had never asked.

Jane Sanderson asked, so I told her. That was in 1990 and *People* was doing a story about the new Tammy Wynette, the made-over Tammy who had a new look and was taking her music in new directions. She had booked 142 concert dates that year. The article would rehash her stormy life and spectacular successes and the strains her career had placed on her family.

In fact, it was Tammy who brought up the subject of

frayed mother-daughter relationships, which the reporter, naturally, felt compelled to explore.

In talking about her aborted 1986 stay at the Betty Ford Center, where she was being treated for addiction to pain medicine, Mom said, "I tell my children, 'I never took cocaine, marijuana or speed. I just took something to ease pain.' They blame me, but they've never endured pain. They've never had an operation and don't know how to sympathize."

Blame? From that, the magazine writer sensed there was trouble in the Wynette clan and asked me and my sisters about it.

I was twenty-eight then and still harboring resentment, but not stemming from her addiction to painkillers. I regretted her dependence and worried about where it was leading her, but I resented her long absences during my childhood and adolescence.

Gwen and Tina were the most embittered, but I wasn't far behind. But I—more than my sisters, who had no children at the time of our *People* interview—was willing to forgive because I wanted my mother in my life and wanted my daughters to know their grandmother. I loved Mom, and at some point I realized I could love her despite her failings.

Even then, it took a lot of years for me to realize that I may have judged her too severely. Mom spent her life on the road for two reasons: she loved the lifestyle and she craved the financial security it afforded her and her children. I think those motives carried equal weight.

I was too young by the time we left that log cabin with no running water to appreciate the environment we'd left behind, where our lives weren't poverty-stricken so much as monotonous. By the time I was old enough to start school, Tammy Wynette was on her way to becoming a big star. I grew up in homes that most people would consider mansions, and life was anything but routine. As most children would, I suppose, I took the wealth and opulence for granted, so it did not temper my judgment of my mother. I simply felt that she placed her career—being a star, a celebrity—above her children.

It was far more complex than that.

Now I am a mother, a single mother with four daughters. I have a deep yearning to give them the best. I understand the sleepless nights parents spend fretting over their children's futures, obsessed with their well-being. I understand that maternal desire to provide security—materially and emotionally. And I know how hard that security is to come by, particularly for a single mother. I've gained a deeper appreciation for my mother. In retrospect, I believe she regretted her absences as much as we did.

MOM HAD MARRIED my father, Euple Byrd, just a few months shy of her eighteenth birthday and divorced him five and a half years later. It was only then that the singing aspirations of her childhood and teenage years were revived.

Gwen was four years old, I was three, and Tina, who had been born prematurely and nearly died from spinal meningitis four months later, was not yet half a year old, but we were about to become veterans of the road, and Mom's old car would seem more like home than the small apartments we rented.

When she left my dad, Mom moved us to Birmingham, where she had family on her father's side, and quickly found a job as a beauty operator. One of her uncles was the chief engineer for WBRC-TV, which aired a music show called *Country Boy Eddie* early every weekday morning. Mom watched it regularly—actually, she listened to it more than she watched, while she was getting ready for work—and so she was aware that there were no "girl singer" regulars on the show and very few female guests.

She persuaded her uncle Harvey to help her get an audition, and she was hired on the spot. I think that's when my sisters and I began adjusting to life with an absentee mother. Mom would get up at four every morning, drive across town to appear on *Country Boy Eddie,* then drive back across town to the beauty salon and work until seven each night.

Her daughters were consigned mostly to the loving care of her aunts and cousins.

That little gig on Birmingham television soon turned into something bigger and, I suppose, better. She began to meet radio disc jockeys and bit players on the fringes of country music. She even landed a temporary job with Porter Wagoner, opening for him on a ten-day tour through Alabama and Georgia.

She often said that was the biggest thrill of her life, up to that time, but the pivotal experience came a few months later.

Through disc-jockey friends, she made her first trip to Nashville in 1965, during the city's biggest week of the year—the annual Disc Jockey Convention and the Country Music awards banquet.

That was her first time to sing at the Ryman Auditorium—not in the Ryman, but outside of it, on a flatbed truck where a country band was playing and a radio station owner was inviting anyone to sing.

If Virginia Wynette Pugh Byrd had any doubts about

where her life was headed, that experience resolved them. There was no huge ovation—truth was, the crowd largely ignored her—but the snake had bitten and the venom would forever be in her blood.

After that, she was running up to Nashville every chance she got, knocking on doors on Music Row, but for months all she had to show for it was sore knuckles. In January of 1966, we made the move, Mom and Gwen and Tina and I, and all of our belongings, packed like sausages into her 1956 Chevrolet.

Mom rented a room in an old motel and, since we had no relatives in Nashville, she'd load us girls into the car and take us with her as she made the rounds of record producers. In fact, we were waiting in the car the day she walked into Epic Records and met Billy Sherrill, who listened to her sing one song and told her he would record her if she could come up with a good song.

Early the next morning, we were all back in the car making the rounds of publishing companies, looking for the song that would launch my mother's career. She found one that she liked and took it to Billy Sherrill the next day. He was unimpressed and promised to call her if he found something better.

Days passed and finally Mom called him.

"Come to my office," he said. "I've got something I want you to hear."

We all piled back in the car and raced down to Epic Records. I guess Gwen and I were starting to think this was what life would always be: bouncing around the streets of a strange city in a ten-year-old Chevy, pausing long enough for Mom to duck into one building or another and come out with a long face.

That day, she came out smiling. She had a song, "Apartment #9," and a new name.

Virginia Wynette Byrd didn't have the right resonance, Sherrill told her; it just didn't fit her.

"What does fit me?" she asked him.

"With that blond ponytail, you look like a Tammy to me."

A star was born.

ONE OF THE cruelties of the recording business is that you can drive along hearing your hit song on the radio and still not have enough money in your pocket to buy a tank of gas. The expenses of making a record—the studio time, musicians and everything else—are charged to the artist, and those expenses have to be paid before the artist begins receiving royalties.

"Apartment #9" wasn't a chart-topper, but it did pretty well, making the Top 40, and it launched Mom's career, but the money seemed a long time coming. As often as she could, Mom would leave us girls with a relative while she traveled to personal appearances. A lot of times, she took us along. Most of what I remember about those trips is the view from that car, the world flitting past the backseat window.

Often, before we'd drive off, Mom would pack a big box of food—fried chicken and potato salad or baked ham and dumplings—and we would spread a blanket on the grass beside the highway and eat our picnic lunch.

It wasn't long, though, before Gwen and I were old enough for school and traveling became impractical. By then, Mom could afford to pay someone to look after us.

From that point on, my sisters and I were reared by a string of nannies and governesses, some of whom we liked and some we didn't. Mostly, they were nothing more than baby-sitters who would get us off to school, make us do our homework, feed us, see that we bathed and got to bed on time. They were not tutors (one was a young Vietnamese refugee who spoke little English) or skilled at guiding young girls across the trip wires of childhood.

It seemed that those we liked never stayed around long enough, while those we didn't like hung on, no matter how hard we tried to make their lives unpleasant.

When our schedules permitted, we would go on tour with Mom or fly to wherever she was performing and spend a little time with her. Then there were the brief periods—usually early in the week—when she would come home between shows. Entertainers usually work weekends, so Mom's days off normally were school days for us. I honestly think she wanted to be a mother and tried hard to be one, but there were just too many demands on her time for the first fifteen years of her singing career.

I remember one occasion when Gwen, Tina and I were teenagers and Mom came in from the road. She had the weekend off, and she called all the girls together to discuss what she had planned for the next few days.

She was crushed when we informed her we had already made our own plans for the weekend. When Mom was displeased with us, she didn't always express it verbally. But she would make a long, pouting face that we learned to read pretty well.

Gwen told her, "What do you think we do when you're gone—sit around here and miss Mama?"

Mom started to say something, but I interrupted.

"Don't ever worry about us adjusting to your being away so much. It's the only life we know and we've learned to handle it."

That may have been the first time my mother realized something important: that her daughters had grown up without her. Her children had found their own way while she was looking in the other direction.

That weekend, she got in her car and drove down to Florida. Along the way, she wrote a poem to us:

Dear Daughters:
Gwen, you're my oldest. You're quite a lady,
My only blue-eyed girl.
You turned sixteen in April
And you sure made a change in my world.
I'm sorry I missed the big evening,
Your first date and I wasn't around.
Save all the secret things you did
And tell me when I get to town.
And on your graduation, I wanted pictures to look
     back on.
But I wasn't there to take them.
As usual I was gone.
You've had to grow up much too quick
And you've done it your own way.
You did it without Mama
'Cause Mama wasn't home.

And, Jackie, you're quite a lady, too.
You're just one year younger than Gwen.
And there's so much that I'm missing
By being Mommy now and then.

I remember the day you cooked your first meal.
You were nine; you cooked biscuits and ham.
You called to tell me how good it was,
'Cause I was out of town.
And at the party for fathers and daughters
I know you felt out of place.
Even the pretty dress I bought
Couldn't fill that empty space.
And the time when you got sick
And the doctor turned you down;
He said they couldn't treat you
With your Mama out of town.

And Tina, you're such a pretty girl
With big almond eyes of brown.
They voted you homecoming queen
While I was out of town.
I know you were a beauty
'Cause your sisters dress you right,
And you said it didn't matter
That I couldn't be there that night.
And the day you joined the cheerleading team
Nothing could hold you down.
You yelled "Hip, hip hooray" over the phone
'Cause as usual, I was out of town.

And Tamala Georgette Jones,
You simply take my breath away.
Born just six short years ago
And named for your daddy and me.
Going to sleep on MeeMaw's arm, listening to her
*   hum,*

Drifting off to Fairyland
While sucking on your thumb.
Just yesterday you pulled a tooth.
Boy, you sure are brave and strong.
I wish I could have been there
But as usual, I was gone.

She gave a copy of the poem to us, but she also gave it to her audiences. She regularly recited that poem during her concerts and it wasn't unusual for women in the audience to weep. Mom wanted people to know that the life of a famous singer wasn't all glamour. She wanted them to know that she was a real person with real problems and that there was a price to be paid for being Tammy Wynette or anyone else in a comparable position.

In 1983, Mom was at the DJ Convention at the Opryland Hotel and she met Naomi Judd, who was just breaking into the business. Naomi and Wynonna had signed with RCA Records, but they were still new to Nashville and looking a little lonely at the convention.

Mom, on the other hand, was the center of attention as soon as she walked into the room. Naomi didn't have the courage to approach her, but they eventually found themselves standing near each other. Mom struck up a conversation.

"You know," Naomi said, "one of my kids and I are going to buy a bus and go out on the road, and the other one is going to get left at home. What can you tell me about what it's like to be a woman on the road with a kid at home?"

All of a sudden, my mom was transformed. She wasn't a big star anymore, just a mother. She talked about her daughters and how difficult it was being away from us, monitoring our lives through phone calls from truck stops across America.

"You're going to miss birthday parties and proms, and she's going to be mad at you, but you'll be able to put her through college and give her a great lifestyle. That's what keeps me going all the time."

$\mathcal{S}ix$

MY GRANDMOTHER MILDRED, whom all the grandchildren called "MeeMaw," was strict with her daughter, but probably not any stricter than other parents in the rural South in those days. Part of her overprotectiveness may have come from her late entry into her daughter's life.

By the time MeeMaw returned from years of work at that defense plant in Memphis, Mom was approaching her teens. Much of what would be her adult nature had already been formed, but MeeMaw no doubt still viewed her as a child.

Mom wasn't a bad child. She probably wasn't even any wilder than an average young girl, but MeeMaw hadn't had much experience with raising a child or setting appropriate limitations for one. And, Virginia Wynette Pugh, even as a child, had a daring streak, a stubbornness that could cause a mother to sit up nights.

More than once she was caught sneaking her grandmother's snuff out to the well house and getting violently sick on it. One time, she and her friend Jane Williams tricked a neighborhood bully into drinking a mixture of white clay and water by convincing him that it was milk. No real harm was done, and he never pestered them again.

One story that Mom often told on herself, without shame, was about the stunt she pulled that destroyed the cotton gin.

A county fair opened in Tupelo on a Saturday, and her grandpa told her that if she picked fifty pounds of cotton before noon, she could have the rest of the day off to go to the fair.

She had been picking cotton since she was six or seven years old, so she knew how to work her way down a row in a hurry, but that Saturday, she decided to hedge a little, just to be sure she got to the fair.

She started before sunrise and when noon rolled around, she was certain that her sack didn't weigh fifty pounds. So, she weighted it with rocks, something a lot of cotton pickers have tried but have rarely gotten away with because the scales will usually reveal the scam.

She failed spectacularly—and she wasn't caught by an audit.

Putting rocks in a load of cotton was dangerous because they can strike the metal parts of the gin and cause sparks. After weighing her sack, Mom took it behind the wagon and tried to remove all the rocks. She missed one, and, sure enough, when that load was sucked from the wagon into the gin, rock and metal clashed and sparked, sending three hundred pounds of cotton up in flames. She had to pick that much cotton, without pay, to compensate for the damage.

But it was over boys that she and her mother collided most seriously.

Her mother had remarried when Mom was four, to a

gentleman named Foy Lee, whom my mother came to idolize. Mom continued living with her grandparents, though, until she was about fourteen. When she moved in with her mother and stepfather, the friction began almost immediately.

Foy, who became "PeePaw" to us grandchildren, often defended Mom when he thought MeeMaw was being too harsh or strict with her. But when the issue was boys, MeeMaw was unyielding. She came from that backwoods, Southern Baptist culture which held sins of the flesh to be the worst sins of all. MeeMaw got that from her parents. When Mom was living with her grandparents and playing basketball in school, her grandpa thought the uniforms were immorally skimpy, so he made her wear jeans during games. Eventually, he relented and allowed her to wear the regulation shorts, but only after her grandma had sewn elastic around the legs to ensure that her panties would not be exposed.

It is not surprising, therefore, that talk about sex was taboo in that environment, especially when the discussion was to be with one's children. So as mother reached that age when she first grew curious about the opposite sex, she had no parental guidance in intimate matters. MeeMaw's course was to avoid direct discussion of the subject, while continuing to fret over it in private. I think she believed that if she could just keep Mom away from boys, everything would be fine.

It wouldn't be that easy.

Mom was drawn to boys like chickens to corn. She used to laugh about falling in love with Billy Cole in the sixth grade and by the ninth grade being determined to marry him, although they had only been together in church or on double dates with Linda Cayson and Billy's brother. She was only fifteen years old (Billy was nineteen), and, being impulsive as she was, probably had not thought through the seriousness of matrimony. She just wanted to get married and be on her own, and she was naive enough to think she could pull it off without her mother finding out.

Fat chance in a small community. She and Billy bought mail-order rings for $8 apiece and had them delivered to her school. Then, of course, she couldn't restrain herself from sharing the good news with all her friends. When all the girls in a tiny school know something, you can bet the teachers will soon get wind of it. And, when the teachers know, the parents know.

MeeMaw quickly shut down the wedding plans, which made Mom even more resentful of her interfering mother, who meddled even more as Mom got older. Curfews were rigidly imposed, and if Mom came in a few minutes late, she was questioned and accused. When she went on dates, her parents would sometimes appear, dropping in at a café or drive-in movie or baseball game where they knew Mom and her date would be. When one of her classmates got pregnant, Mom was forbidden to associate with her.

By the time she was a senior, she was popular enough to be voted Miss Tremont High and have a string of boys lining up to date her. But her mother was always circling in the background, stepping forward long enough to chase away the boys she didn't like and controlling Mom's social life like a cruise director.

It was about that time that Mom met my father, Euple Byrd. He was several years older than she and had been away in the Army, which, in her eyes, gave him a sophisticated and worldly aura.

MeeMaw didn't approve of him, but he was one beau she couldn't chase away. He and my mom came home from a date half an hour late once and MeeMaw told Mom she could never see him again, because "he doesn't respect you enough to get you home on time."

"I will see him," Mom shouted. "If I can't see him any other way, I'll marry him."

A violent argument ensued. It ended with MeeMaw hitting Mom in the mouth with a belt hard enough to draw blood.

Mom went to a friend's house to spend the night and the friend's mother tried to talk her out of doing something she would regret. *You don't get married because you're angry at your mother,* she counseled. *You have to really love the person you're marrying.*

"Well," Mom said, "I will love him."

When I think of that incident now, I realize that those words explain a lot of the troubles in Mom's life. She wanted desperately to escape the intractable supervision of her mother, and, as it seemed to many young women of that era, escape was spelled h-u-s-b-a-n-d.

I don't know if she ever truly learned to love my father, and if she didn't, she also did not learn the lesson of marrying for the wrong reasons.

HER MEMORIES OF her wedding day always had a school-girlish quality to them, and why not? She was still a schoolgirl—one month shy of graduating from high school—when she and Euple Byrd slipped off to Fulton, Mississippi, for a quickie ceremony in the home of a preacher they found in the phone book.

She often laughed about that day in the way that young girls might giggle while describing their first kiss to a slumber party of girlfriends.

She was still just seventeen and needed parental consent to get a marriage license. Her mother would not sign the papers, so her stepfather, as he had done so many times, intervened on her behalf. I think now that he either felt she was old enough, or that getting away from her mother was a good idea; or perhaps he knew her well enough to know that if he didn't sign the consent papers she would lie about her age and get married anyway. Parental sanction, for whatever reason it was given, might prevent further alienation. PeePaw had grown close to Mom and, I believe, he wanted her to remain a part of his family.

So, with PeePaw's blessing, she and my father lit out for Fulton, were married, drove immediately back to Tremont and went straight to the high school to tell her friends what they had done. "That was the most exciting part of the day," she once said.

No wonder. They apparently didn't plan much beyond the ceremony.

By nightfall, she learned that marriage in and of itself did not guarantee the liberation she craved. She and her new husband had no place to live, so his family put them up for a while. Then, married less than six months and expecting their first child, they moved back in with Mildred and Foy, back into the household she had schemed so mightily to escape.

Her pregnancy may have helped patch the rift between her and her mother. MeeMaw was excited about having a grandchild and gave Mom a lot of support, including helping her and Euple get settled in the old cabin on her Grandpa Russell's farm.

Even if she married my father for the wrong reason, I am convinced that Mom was determined to make it work. In her autobiography she wrote that she had imagined that marriage would be accompanied by a vine-covered cottage with starched white curtains blowing in the breeze (I think some part of that vision followed her throughout her life), but instead, she had a drafty cabin with an outhouse and a stove that didn't work. But she didn't lose heart or bail out. She worked long hours to make that place a home and conceived her second child there.

My father drifted from one menial job to another and, by Mom's account, showed little inclination to settle into one career and stay put. After I was born, we moved to Red Bay, but after three months, Dad was out of work, so we moved on to Memphis. In spite of the disappointment she must have felt, Mom followed dutifully, even willingly, wherever Dad's nomadic urge took them.

Maybe she felt that she had no choice. It was either stick with her husband or go back to her mother's home with hat in hand. Her unwillingness to do that is something I admire. She had dealt her own cards, so she would play the hand.

It turned out that Memphis would be pivotal ground for her.

We lived in a small apartment in a seedy part of town, but she regularly took Gwen and me out for an airing. Walking along Front Street one afternoon, she paused outside a tavern to listen to the piano music coming from inside. The owner spotted us standing on the sidewalk and came outside and struck up a conversation. She offered Mom a job as a barmaid.

Slinging drinks led to singing along with the piano player, which led to customers offering generous tips for her to sing their favorites. One night, Carl, the pianist, awoke the beast that had long hibernated in her bosom. "You belong in Nashville," he told her.

By then, it seemed an impossible dream. She had two children and a husband who changed jobs and addresses every few months. She had attended school to learn beauty-salon work and it must have seemed to her that her lot was irrevocable. Fixing hair. Raising babies. Relocating.

Finally, in 1965, after we had moved once again back to Tremont, she had had enough. Twenty-three years old, sick with a kidney infection and pregnant with Tina, she told Dad she wanted a divorce and ordered him out of our apartment.

That was the beginning of an ordeal that might have destroyed a young woman of lesser grit. Along with the persistent kidney problem, she fell into a depression so pernicious that her doctor decided to treat it with shock therapy. Without my father's financial support, we had to move to an efficiency apartment, and because Dad had taken the car, we had no transportation until she went to work as a receptionist for a doctor, who loaned her $200 to buy an old Chevy.

One night, when we went to visit one of Mom's friends, someone broke into our apartment and looted it. They took everything, our food, clothes, dishes, furniture, everything. Mom was convinced that Dad was responsible, but before she could even report it to the police, the police came to the door and arrested her and took all three of us to the police station. Dad had gone to the juvenile authorities and alleged that Mom was unstable and unfit to care for Gwen and me.

It took all night for her to convince them that she was sane and a fit mother. We all went back to that bare efficiency and slept on the floor.

Probably the worst part, though, was that Mom's decision to divorce renewed the acrimony between her and her mother, who viewed divorce as a disgrace for the entire family. I don't know if MeeMaw really liked my father, but she became his devoted ally when he resisted the divorce.

A couple of weeks after the apartment burglary, Dad and MeeMaw came by the nursery school and picked up me and Gwen. Mom had always picked us up before, but we were too young to imagine that anything was amiss. It was just our father and our grandmother.

When Mom came to get us that day and found that we were gone, she was more angry than frightened. From the description of the man and woman who had taken us away, she knew immediately who it was. For six days, she was unable to locate Dad. She repeatedly called MeeMaw, who just as repeatedly denied knowing where we were.

Frustrated, she left work early one afternoon and drove to MeeMaw's house, thinking she could persuade her mother to tell her where Dad was hiding out. She didn't get a chance to have that conversation. She didn't need to.

When she pulled into the driveway, she saw Gwen and me playing in the front yard. Dad's car was in the garage. Before anyone knew she was there, she herded Gwen and me into her car and peeled out of the driveway. Dad chased us into Tupelo but drove on when she stopped at the courthouse.

The very next day, she quit her job and called her grandparents, William and Margaret Pugh, in Birmingham. Two weeks later, we were in her old Chevy with all of our worldly goods, headed away from Tupelo and Tremont and Red Bay for the last time.

The first stop was Birmingham, where Tina was born and also my mother's singing career.

In less than two years, we would be in Nashville and Mom would have her contract with Epic Records. "Apartment #9" would be beamed from radio stations across America.

Seven

AFTER HER UNHAPPY experience with my father, you would think that Mom would have learned something about men and relationships; but she had a weakness that revisited her each and every time there was no man in her life. She simply did not like to be alone, did not like to sleep alone. That, too, may have been a sensibility molded on the farm.

Until she was thirteen or so, she lived with her grandparents, who had separate bedrooms. Mom usually slept with her grandfather. That may seem odd now, but in those days farm families lived like that. Sleeping two and three to a bed was common, and the age and gender mix didn't seem to matter—up to a point.

In her autobiography, she described the night when that point was reached and the mild trauma that she experienced.

Her grandfather apparently had decided that she was at an age when it was no longer proper for her to share his bed, and he insisted that she move to her aunt Carolyn's room. That abrupt change in nighttime routine left her feeling rejected. She reasoned that she had somehow brought it upon herself.

"I had no idea why he did that or what I'd done wrong," she wrote. "I didn't ask him why. I cried myself to sleep for nights after that. To this day, I can't stand to sleep alone."

Women who were close to her over the years, friends who had watched her careen through one disastrous marriage after another, have told me they believe her vulnerability to ill-fated love stemmed from a primal longing: She was always looking for Daddy, for the father she never had, for the guardian and protector that was always absent from her life. Whenever a man stepped forward with the promise of filling that void, she permitted hope to triumph over reason.

Had she given even casual scrutiny to Euple Byrd, my father, she would have seen that he was not the picket-fenced-and-white-curtained-cottage kind of man. Perhaps she was too young then to be so discerning, but by the time she met Don Chapel, she was old enough to weigh her decision more carefully.

No, hope won out again.

When she began making her periodic trips to Nashville from Birmingham, the first place she went was the Anchor Motel. It was the only place in Nashville she knew to go to, since she had stayed there when she attended that first DJ Convention.

To her, the Anchor might have seemed a fortuitous selection. Don Chapel was the night clerk and, like Mom, was hell-bent on making it as a singer and songwriter. He was still struggling but had family connections: one of his sisters, Martha, was a singer and had at least made it to the minor leagues of country music; another sister, Jean, was a talented writer and a published one to boot.

After we pulled up stakes and made the permanent move to Nashville in 1966, Mom spent a lot of time with Don and Jean, who were very supportive. Jean made the dress that Mom wore to the DJ Convention that year, and Don escorted her to the party.

She needed all the support she could get. "Apartment #9" had been released shortly before that convention and was moving up the charts, but we were still broke, still living in a tourist court, still without the clothes we needed for the approaching winter. Mom kept knocking on doors, trying to get a booking agent who could line up some personal appearances. Royalties from her first record would be slow to arrive, but a live show would be an immediate payday.

Every talent agent she approached turned her down. She was unknown, and besides, they told her, *girl singers* were a lot of trouble. *Girl singers* were not reliable draws. That's the way it was when she arrived in Nashville: there were singers and there were *girl singers,* and the latter clearly were second-class citizens.

Gradually, she began to get some bookings; but the pay wasn't enough to move us out of the tourist court, and during that time, Mom became really fond of Don Chapel and his sister. Jean would baby-sit so Mom and Don could go to a movie, and Jean was eager to give Mom advice or information about the music business.

Mom and Don had a lot in common. Both were divorced and had three children. Both had country-music aspirations and were struggling to realize them. They were comfortable with each other. They were friends.

So, when Don asked Mom to marry him, she accepted

the offer—for the wrong reasons. She never made any bones about her feelings for Don or her motives for marrying him. She admitted she didn't love him but believed that would come later. For the moment, she had a more pressing need. She was now on the road quite a bit and found it exciting but lonely. She didn't like being single.

A year after we moved to Nashville, she and Don drove over to Georgia and were married by a justice of the peace. The parallels to her elopement with my father did not escape her, but the lessons of it did.

As far as I know, she and Don got along fine at first. Her second song, "Your Good Girl's Gonna Go Bad," hit No. 1 on the country charts and was followed by another chart-topper, "I Don't Wanna Play House," which also won a Grammy Award. "My Elusive Dreams," a duet with David Houston, also made it to the top. She was making enough money to buy a $50,000 house on Old Hickory Lake, a house big enough for her three children and Don's three. But success was putting a strain on her marriage.

Don's career as a writer and singer was on the slow track, and there wasn't much Mom could do to push it along. He played guitar and sang a little in her show, but he just couldn't get a toehold, let alone a recording contract.

She was getting bigger by the week and was being booked on bills with the biggest stars in the business, including her idol, George Jones. She even bought her first bus from Jones, and that led to friction between her and Don.

Although it was her show, Don insisted on painting THE DON CHAPEL AND TAMMY WYNETTE SHOW on the side of the bus. She went along with it—he was her husband, after all, and she was just a *girl singer*—but she never accepted it. Don also insisted on singing solos on the show—too many to please the promoters—and Mom was constantly fending off their complaints. He pressured her to persuade Billy Sherrill to record him, but she doubted he could make it as a singer.

He was doing a little better as a songwriter—Jones recorded some of his material—but it was apparent that whatever success he achieved would always be eclipsed by that of his wife. They began to fight a lot—about the show and about the children. They even had a fight over Jones, after he stopped by the house one night to tell them that his divorce from his wife of seventeen years became final that day. Don suspected that Jones had designs on Mom and he told her so.

But Mom always said that the thing that drove her away from Don was her discovery of his secret hobby. Occasionally, he would playfully snap nude pictures of her, when she was preparing for bed or getting out of the shower or something like that. It didn't particularly annoy her until she learned what he was doing with those photographs.

A man showed up at one of her shows and handed her an envelope. During a break, she opened it and saw that it contained one of the nude pictures Don had taken. She confronted her husband and he admitted that he had been swapping nude pictures of her with men whose names he got from advertisements in magazines.

She didn't divorce him immediately. He apologized and promised it would never happen again and she accepted that—at least on the outside. Inside, any feelings she might have had for him were destroyed by that act, which she considered repulsive. Still, she had the same old need, the need for a man, a companion, someone to fill the emotional void that caused her such dread. Don served that purpose, so she stayed with him.

Parting with him may have been difficult for her for another reason—Don's daughter, Donna. She was sixteen when she moved into the house with us, and she and Mom bonded immediately. Donna also wanted to be a singer, and Mom put her in the show, sometimes singing backup for Mom and sometimes singing duets with Don. Rather than pursue a singing career, though, Donna eventually got married and moved away, but she and Mom stayed in touch for years after Don was out of my mother's life.

IN RETROSPECT, IT seems obvious that George Jones was as taken by my mother as she was by him. He was married when they first met, so he didn't make a major-league play for her, but his actions suggested that to him she was more than just a business associate.

After "My Elusive Dreams," her duet with David Houston, became a number-one hit, they were booked on a few shows with Jones. One night, Mom got into an argument with David's manager over some changes he wanted to make in their routine. The fallout was that she refused to sing the duet. David left early and his manager would not allow Mom to use his band for her part of the show.

Not only did Jones let his band play for her, but when he came on to close the show, he called her back on stage so he could sing "My Elusive Dreams" with her. He didn't even know the words, so she had to prompt him as they went along. The audience loved it, but Mom was downright astounded.

She was having a lot of success in her own right, but she was still in awe of Jones. Singing with him for the first time nearly left her speechless. After the show, she managed to thank him profusely for his help.

"Look," he told her, "I heard what happened. If anything like that happens again on this tour, you let me know. I'll sing duets with you at any time."

Little did she know then that in a very short time, they would be the most celebrated duo in the music world.

Jones already had a reputation as a difficult artist. His drinking binges had earned him the nickname "No Show Jones," and he was a booking agent's nightmare. But to other artists, he was known as a generous and softhearted guy. He was that and more to Tammy Wynette.

That first year she was on the road, Mom and her crew, which consisted of her and Don and Donna and another guitar player, traveled by car. She felt that neither her budget nor her entourage was large enough for a bus, but then she learned that Jones was buying a new one.

"What are you going to do with your old one?" she asked him.

"I'll try to get what I can get out of it," he said.

"How much would that be?" she asked. Because Don had been pressing her to buy a bus, she had asked around and had some idea of the prices. Jones's, she thought, might be worth $20,000.

"For you," Jones said, "it would be two thousand dollars."

She protested that it was worth more than that, but Jones kept repeating, "For you, it's two thousand dollars."

At that price, it was more of a gift than a sale.

One night after Jones's divorce was final, he and Mom finished a show and were talking backstage when he casually asked her where she was going next.

"Red Bay, Alabama," she said. "I spent a lot of my childhood around there and I'm going back to do a benefit and help them raise money to air-condition their new school."

With a blank look on his face, Jones said, "I've never heard of Red Bay."

She got on her bus and headed to Alabama. The next night, she was still sitting in her bus outside the auditorium when a shiny new burgundy Cadillac pulled up and parked beside her. It was the kind of car that was starkly out of place in the Red Bay she remembered. She watched, astounded, as the door opened and Jones got out. He stuck his head through the door of her bus and said, "So this is Red Bay, Alabama."

She gasped, "What are you doing here?"

Jones smiled. "I came to do a benefit. Didn't you tell me they need air-conditioning here?"

For a star of George Jones's wattage to impulsively perform for a small-town benefit certainly was an act of generosity, but it was a lot more than that—it was an act of a man in full pursuit of a woman.

OVER THE YEARS, I've heard rumors that Mom became involved with Jones while she was still married to Don. That's the kind of buzz that entertainment communities thrive on, but if it was true, she never acknowledged it to me in those later years when we talked about such personal things, or talked around the edges of them. In fact, she wrote in her autobiography that when Jones professed his love for her, she was shocked.

I think it's possible that not all of the shock came from

his words. The way in which he revealed his feelings may have contributed to the jolt. Like the knight she had always dreamed of, Jones swept her out of a bad marriage—a kind of heroic rescue—in a very dramatic way.

It happened one night when he came by the house and found Mom and Don in a bitter fight. Their relationship had utterly decayed until there was nothing left of it but a bad odor. They fought all the time, and each fight was more vicious than the last. That night, they couldn't restrain themselves even in the presence of guests. The sniping and bickering went on while Don mixed Jones a drink.

Mom was sitting at the dinner table with her checkbook and bills and a lot of other papers that required her attention. She snapped at Don over something, and he responded by calling her a "bitch."

To say Jones went berserk is an understatement. He grabbed a corner of the table and flipped it over, then picked up a chair and threw it through a plate-glass window. Jones had been drinking that night and could be a violent drunk in those days, but this rage seemed to come from something more profound than alcohol.

"You don't talk to her like that," he screamed at Don.

Like Mom, Don was stunned by what he had just seen. "What's it to you?" he asked, a little hesitantly. "She's my damn wife."

"That may be so," Jones said, "but I love her."

He walked over and stood behind Mom with his hand on her shoulder and said, "And you love me, too, don't you?"

Without pausing to think it over, she blurted out, "Yes, I do."

"Then let's go," he said.

Don stood quietly, dazed, I suppose, as Mom ushered me and Gwen and Tina toward the door. In the car, she turned once to see the house disappearing in the night, and she never looked back again.

Eight

THERE'S A LINE in a country song that I think sums up Mom's years with George Jones. *Sometimes it's heaven and sometimes it's hell and sometimes I don't even know.*

She knew about his drinking but she believed he engaged in such destructive behavior because he was sad or lonely or had some other emotional need that was not being met. If she could make him happy, he would have no need for booze or drugs.

For a while, it looked like she was correct.

In 1968, Jones was at his career zenith, and Mom was about to join him on that plateau. She had recorded a song she wrote with Billy Sherrill in about twenty minutes during a recording-session break and it was the song that would define her career, if not her personal life. "Stand by Your Man" shot to the top of the charts and looked as if it would stay there through the millennium. It also crossed over to the pop charts and made it to the Top 20. That same year "Take Me to Your World" and "D-I-V-O-R-C-E" also

became number-one hits, and Mom was named Female Vocalist of the Year by the Country Music Association.

Their first days together, from Mom's accounts, were
wholly blissful. George gave her a new Lincoln Continen-
tal to replace the car she had left behind when she walked
out of her house with him. He gave her a four-carat dia-
mond ring and they flew to Mexico City to get her divorce
from Don. It was then that Mom got her first taste of the
bitter side of celebrity. When they returned from Mexico,
she saw her private life, for the first time, in the headlines.
TAMMY WYNETTE LEAVES HUSBAND FOR GEORGE JONES,
screamed the *Nashville Banner.*

Then her attorney informed her that the Mexican divorce was worthless in Tennessee, so she had to file a new
petition in Nashville. As her lawyer anticipated, Don filed
a countersuit in which he accused her of desertion and
adultery, which led to more headlines and fortified the rumors that she had been unfaithful to her husband.

In the grand scheme, that was a minor irritation to her,
and being with Jones made it all worthwhile. She had
moved in with him and they were keeping busy separate
schedules and sometimes performing together. In January
1969, they both became members of the Grand Ole Opry,
and a month later, while they were in Atlanta for a joint appearance, they drove over to Ringold and got married.

ABOUT A MONTH after Mom and Jones married, we moved
to Lakeland, Florida, to what Mom hoped would be a new
life. She wanted to get away from Nashville and the minor
scandal that had kicked up over her leaving Don Chapel to
abruptly move in with her childhood idol. Away from the

gossip, she could relax and be a mother. She moved her grandma and grandpa Pugh down from Birmingham, so she could look after them, and later she bought a house nearby for her parents, Mildred and Foy. With kids and parents and grandparents around, she would have a serene counterbalance to the wired music world and the prying press.

Away from the temptations of old haunts and cohorts, she believed, Jones might also wean himself from the bottle.

Georgette was born later that year, and for a while Jones behaved like a changed man. He bought an old plantation house with sixteen rooms and enough land around it to build a country-music entertainment park, a project that he approached with zeal. But, periodically, he would answer to the siren call of the smoke-filled bar, disappearing for days, only to return home full of apologies and promises never to do it again.

Mom didn't nag or reproach him, not at first. She was in love and confident that love would conquer his drinking. On a vacation trip, she sent a photograph of her and Jones and Georgette, with Niagara Falls in the background, to her old friend Linda Cayson. On the back she'd written, *Lin, all of my dreams have finally come true.*

In a sense, so had mine.

Jones wasn't merely *like* a father to me and my sisters, he *was* our father. We had had no contact with our natural father since moving to Nashville, and, while we got along great with Don Chapel and his kids, we were not with them long enough for real familial bonds to form.

With Jones it was different. If he and Mom fought, they didn't do it in our presence. And Jones was not the self-centered egomaniac that a lot of superstars become. In fact, his career did not seem to make even the Top 5 on his list of priorities.

After Georgette was born, he legally adopted Gwen, Tina and me. He was away a lot, as was Mom, but when he was around, he spent time with us, took us places, and played games with us. He never spanked us, never even raised his voice to us. If we even hinted that we wanted something, he saw to it that we got it. It was almost always fun when he was around.

He was the same toward Mom and his friends.

Jan Smith, Mom's hairdresser, has told me something that Jones did after we left Florida and moved back to Nashville. Jan sold her house in Nashville and moved to Atlanta. After a few months, she decided she didn't like it there and wanted to move back, but she had no place to live. She moved in with her sister, Nan, and was living in the attic. When Mom learned of that, she insisted that Jan live with us until she could get a house of her own.

One afternoon, Jones said, "Jan, you can't buy your house back, but what if you had a lot in that same neighborhood?"

"That would probably be okay."

"Go in there and look in my desk and look in that file marked 'Tyne Boulevard.' Bring me that deed."

She got the file and brought it to him. He signed the deed over to her. The lot, Jan estimated, was probably worth $75,000.

After she was settled into her own house, Jan called one day to ask Mom for the name of a good yardman. The phone number had been changed, and since the new one was unlisted, it took Jan a while to find someone who knew it. When she finally got it, she called and Jones answered the phone.

"Dammit," she said, "you changed your number and didn't give it to me."

"Didn't want you to have it," Jones said curtly, and hung up. That was his way of being playful.

Jan called back and talked to Mom, who subsequently scolded Jones for hanging up on Jan. "She was calling about a yardman," she told him.

A little later, Jan got a call from Mom, who said, "Look outside."

Jan turned toward the front window and saw Jones mowing her lawn. "He Stopped Loving Her Today" had just been released and was a huge hit. The sight of the man who had recorded it cutting her grass and raking her leaves sent Jan into a fit of laughter.

When she had settled down, Mom told her, "Don't offer him water or anything."

It was a hot day, but for three hours Jones cut and trimmed and edged the entire yard, and then swept the driveway.

Yard work was probably his favorite domestic activity. Georgette has told me that her earliest memories of her father were of him cranking that mower up on a hot summer day and sitting her on his lap as he tooled around the yard.

Riding mowers became something of an icon in the legend of George Jones.

To keep him from leaving the house to go drinking, Jones's second wife, Shirley, once hid his car keys. Later, she couldn't find him and realized he had left the house—on foot, she assumed. She drove around the neighborhood looking for him and finally found him in a saloon two miles away. She knew he was in the bar because his riding mower was parked outside.

TO A LOT of the country-music community, and certainly to most country-music fans, the partnership of George Jones and Tammy Wynette was the stuff of mythology. Separately, as entertainers, they were blessed with marvelous talents; together they were pure magic. Their voices melded as few twosomes had ever done, and they sang heartrending lyrics that seemed to be straight from their own lives.

If there was a dark side, it was Jones's endless bouts with drink, the binges that lasted for weeks—periods when he would disappear with one crony or another, and neither Mom nor his booking agents or concert promoters would know where he was. Mom endured his lapses longer than most wives would have, standing by him with the hope that one fine day he would get straight.

To me, though, that was not the real dark side of their six-year marriage. Something far worse than a wayward husband attached itself to Tammy Wynette during those years—something that would plague her to the end of her life.

After Georgette was born in 1970, Mom had a couple of surgeries—first an appendectomy and then a hysterectomy. Apparently she didn't heal properly on the inside. Adhesions, and later keloids, formed in her lower abdomen, causing a number of complications, including bowel obstructions and severe pain. Adhesions, according to my medical dictionary, are *fibrous bands of scar tissue that bind together normally separate anatomical structures.*

Keloids are *raised, red formations of fibrous scar tissue caused by excessive tissue repair.*

What that means to me is that the adhesions left by the surgery were causing tissue in her body that should have been separated to fuse together, and repeated attempts to correct the problem only made it worse by creating scar tissue that was just as painful. Over the next twenty-five years, Mom would undergo more than thirty operations, none of which solved her problem.

Some of that may have been her fault. At the time of the hysterectomy, she had what may have been the busiest schedule of her life. She refused to take time to heal before going back on the road. There were a couple of reasons for that. Her star had risen exponentially after "Stand by Your Man." That meant expenses were constant, even if revenues were not. She and Jones had a band, roadies, drivers, pilots, a whole cast of employees who were dependent on them for paychecks. Mom wasn't just singing, either. She kept the books and, a lot of the time, she cooked for the whole crew when they were touring.

And there was another reason she pushed herself so hard. Jones still had his habit of not showing up for dates. How he got away with it is beyond me, but he did. He would come back for a rescheduled show and sheepishly apologize to the audience for previously standing them up.

"I got drunk," he would explain with a grin.

Country-music fans can be very forgiving. In fact, they will forgive about anything but hypocrisy, and Jones was never a hypocrite. He never lied and said he was ill. He never lied and said the bus broke down or the flight was delayed. He never blamed anything or anyone but himself. *I got drunk.* End of excuse.

Mom, though, felt obligated to compensate for his delinquency, or at least avoid being dragged down by it herself. If they had a booking and Jones couldn't or wouldn't go on, she would do the show alone. Sometimes, she took flak from promoters or from audiences, but she was determined to give them their money's worth—even when her health was flagging. No matter how bad her abdominal pains were, she went on stage and showed no sign of discomfort.

As the pain grew worse, her doctors prescribed injections of Demerol, a highly addictive drug with pronounced withdrawal symptoms—one of which is stomach pain. Thus began a merciless cycle: the Demerol would ease her abdominal pains, and when she began to crave it, it would cause them. Thus, while the country-music world was preoccupied with George Jones's whiskey problems, Tammy Wynette was being drawn into a dependency just as pernicious, just as disabling, just as dominating.

There are some doctors who will go to great lengths to placate their celebrity patients, and Mom had more than her share of them in the beginning. One reputable physician even showed Jan Smith how to administer the Demerol injections, advising her how to buy syringes without a prescription. At the same time, she was getting prescriptions for Valium, which is more of a sedative than a painkiller. I don't think those doctors are evil or corrupt; some are just starstruck. They like circling in the orbit of celebrity—rubbing elbows and clinking glasses with the famous. They become enablers, even accomplices to the addiction.

"Tammy Wynette was an addict created by doctors," Jan Smith once told me.

It is curious to me now that she did not recognize what

was happening to her. In those days, her primary vice was cigarettes. Her drinking was limited to an occasional margarita, and while she admitted to trying marijuana a few times, she was adamantly antidrug. If she had caught anyone in her crew using speed or cocaine or heroin, they would have been off the bus immediately.

Painkillers were another matter. She thought of them as medicine, not dope. For the first several years, I don't think she recognized her own dependence. When she felt pain, she thought it was natural to chase it away. Her friends also did not recognize it as a problem, at least not right away. At first, she took small increments, just a few milligrams a day, but as her tolerance increased, she needed larger and larger doses to ward off the withdrawal symptoms.

Friends like Jan Smith and Nan Crafton began to worry when Mom started calling on them to help her get Demerol. Some of the doctors who had dispensed prescriptions freely in the beginning began to refuse her treatment when they realized that she was probably taking Demerol to feed her habit, not kill her pain.

"The doses kept getting larger and larger," Jan told me. "I would give her a shot and she would say, 'That's not enough. If I can't feel it hit the back of my throat, it isn't enough.'"

With the local doctors less and less cooperative, Mom would recruit Jan to cruise the hospital emergency rooms with her, picking up whatever she could con from the attendants. "Some nights, we would go to five hospitals before we had enough to please her," Jan said.

From time to time, her friends would try to discuss her increasing dependence with her, but she would not acknowledge that there was a problem. Denial is the scourge of addiction, and Mom had convinced herself that Demerol was no more than a superstrong aspirin that made the hurt go away. Isn't that what medical science was for?

AFTER THREE YEARS at the Old Plantation Park, we moved back to Nashville, and for the next couple of years, Mom and Jones were the hottest act in country music. Business was good, but life was lousy. Jones's drinking spells were unabated and Mom's forbearance wore thin.

Neither one wanted a divorce and they thrashed around for straws to grasp. Thinking new surroundings might salvage them, they bought an enormous house on Franklin Road—17,500 square feet, fifteen baths, twelve bedrooms, two dens and an Olympic-size pool.

They recorded a hit duet, "We're Gonna Hold On (to Each Other)," but life refused to imitate art.

In December 1975, Jones left on another of his drinking binges, and this time Mom would not let him come back. They divorced a few months later.

Nine

THROUGHOUT MOM'S YEARS with Jones, Goerge Richey was always around. He and his wife, Sheila, were a part of the tide of friends that ebbed and flowed through our houses in Nashville and in Florida. All I knew about him was that he was a songwriter and a musician and record producer. Almost everyone in the business considered him a musical genius. He was the musical director of the television show *Hee Haw* for a long time and had written some songs for Jones, a couple of which were big hits.

After Mom's divorce, he seemed to be around even more. He came by frequently to check on her when she went through a period of serious depression and insomnia. Gwen and I appreciated his attention and concern, especially when Mom had to be rushed to the hospital from an overdose of pills. She had taken several sleeping pills and topped them off with a couple of Valium.

Gwen and I were fourteen and thirteen, respectively,

and didn't know how to handle her. Her two previous divorces had not been particularly traumatic for her, but this one was different. This was a parting with a man she genuinely loved. Their personal lives and professions were tightly intertwined and Mom wasn't sure what she would do without Jones in either capacity.

Jones didn't seem to be taking the parting any better. He moved to Muscle Shoals, Alabama, a little resort area near Florence on the Tennessee River, about 250 miles from Nashville. Often, sometimes several times a week, he would drive to Nashville and circle through the driveway of the house on Franklin Road and then drive back to Alabama—a five-hundred-mile round trip. He later confided to Mom about those obsessive journeys.

"Why did you do it?" she asked.

"Just to see if I was really gone," he said.

I guess it inspired Mom. She wrote two songs—"I Just Drove By (to See If I Was Really Gone)" and "These Days I Barely Get By," which Jones recorded.

Richey was at the hospital when she finally woke up the day after the overdose, and he pleaded with her not to mess around with pills again. Sometimes, he came by to take me or Gwen shopping or to some school activity. He and Sheila even came over the night Mom and a group of her friends were stripping the house of George Jones's memories and mementos.

It's no secret now that his motivation was deeper than friendship. Richey has told everyone, including the tabloids, that he had loved Tammy from afar for years, but that his marriage to Sheila had prohibited him from acting on those feelings.

* * *

MOM NEEDED ALL the moral support she could get in those first months of 1975. She was still at the top of her game professionally. "Stand by Your Man" became a number-one British pop hit and she was starting to think about writing her autobiography. Still, she was astonishingly insecure. Gwen and I, never big country-music fans, were oblivious to her stature in that industry, but what is surprising to me now is that even Mom didn't comprehend how big she was.

"She was not impressed with Tammy Wynette," Jan Smith has told me. "She didn't know she was a big star."

Throughout the most glorious years of her career, she had seen herself as an appendage to . . . what? . . . a man. She was just a girl singer, second bill in the Don Chapel and Tammy Wynette Show or the George Jones and Tammy Wynette Show. No matter how obvious the evidence to the contrary, she was locked into that vision of herself.

One piece of evidence that should have clued her in involved the band that had backed her and Jones for six years. You could say that in the divorce settlement, she got custody of The Jones Boys. By their election.

Mom had a show coming up in Dothan, Alabama, and she fretted for days about working solo. "I don't know what's going to happen," she told Jan Smith. "What if they all just come to see Jones?"

With that on her mind, she began trying to hire a band, only to discover she already had one. One by one, the Jones Boys called to see if she could use their talents. Jones had become so erratic that they feared for their incomes. Whatever else she may have been, Mom was reliable.

At her shows for the next few months, she introduced her band, now called The Country Gentlemen, with the explanation, "This is my half of the property settlement."

* * *

FOR THE NEXT year, things seemed to go well for Mom. She hadn't gotten over Jones completely, but new men kept coming into her life and she was enjoying herself. Most of her romances were well publicized, especially those with Rudy Gatlin, who, with his brothers and sisters, sang backup for her; Tommy Neville, a professional football player; and Burt Reynolds. Except for Reynolds, they were casual flings, I believe, and not serious romances, but they filled Mom's emotional need for a man in her life. Jones even came around now and then, and there seemed to be no lingering rancor between him and Mom. They even agreed to record another duet, "Golden Ring," which was written especially for them by Billy Sherrill and George Richey.

Although she had hired a young Vietnamese woman to be a governess for her daughters, she was at home a lot more, usually in jeans and a casual blouse with her hair tucked inside a bandanna or some cloth wrapped around her head like a turban. Our friends would come to the house and she would prepare snacks, even dinner, for as large a group as we could assemble. She was happy.

That period, however, was marred by a series of bizarre and terrifying incidents that have not been explained to this day.

We started getting nuisance phone calls, sometimes thirty a night. The caller never said anything, just breathed heavily into the phone. Then someone began breaking into the house when we were away, never taking anything but leaving ample evidence that they had been there. Once, we found the skylight open and cigarette butts on the roof. Another time, we came home and the house was flooded. The intruder had put the stopper in the kitchen sink and turned the faucet on full blast. Another night, rocks were thrown through two windows while we were at home.

One night, everyone was in bed and the house was dark, but I was thirsty and got up and went to the kitchen. I could hear two men talking just outside the window. I was petrified and stood there for what seemed like an hour, listening to the men debate where to break into the house. Finally, I ran to Mom's room and woke her up. Just as we got back downstairs to the kitchen, a large rock came crashing through the window.

We called the police each time, but the harassment continued—in fact, accelerated. PIG and WHORE and SLUT were scrawled in red paint and lipstick on our doors, inside and out, and on mirrors and brick walls. Threatening notes— *Tammy Wynette will die*—were placed in our mailbox, and Mom even received death threats while she was on the road. In nine months, there were more than a dozen intrusions into our house, but the police could never find any evidence of a break-in, only a disconnected burglar alarm.

The worst happened in May 1976. Rudy Gatlin had taken us all to a movie that night, and after he had brought us home and departed, we began to hear voices and the sounds of someone prowling around outside. Mom called Rudy and asked him to come back, and bring his gun. He looked around outside, but found nothing.

Mom was determined not to spend the night in that house, so Richey and Sheila invited us to their house. Before we could leave, however, we saw smoke coming from Mom's office. The fire department came and took care of it, but the firemen had barely left when I smelled smoke again. This time it was coming from the trophy room.

When we tried to call the fire department a second time, the phone lines were dead, and we had to summon help from the mobile phone of a reporter who came to the house after hearing about the first fire report. When the firemen returned, they discovered that a fire was raging in a third location—a closet and storage room.

All had been deliberately set, but the fire investigators were convinced that it was an inside job—that one of us had done it. It was even leaked to the newspapers that Rudy Gatlin was a suspect.

What didn't make the newspapers was that all of us were suspects—everyone who lived in the house or had access to it. Gwen was asked to take a lie detector test (which she passed) and I was questioned, along with one of my girlfriends, for hours. Some of our relatives, including my great-grandmother Pugh, were investigated.

The fires, like the intrusions and anonymous phone calls, remained an unsolved mystery, but in time, I would construct my own theory—that someone was trying to terrify my mother for a very specific reason. I thought I knew who it was.

SHE DID IT yet again.

Mom had been dating Burt Reynolds and had even bought a beach house in Jupiter, near where he lived. They met when she appeared on his television show and started seeing each other immediately. I think she really had a thing for him, but she seemed to know that the relationship had no future. Burt was hugely popular and was mobbed by fans everywhere they went. He was funny and charming and she loved being with him, but their identities clashed, at least in her mind. Being married to a big star like George

Jones had not been a problem because they complemented each other, and together they formed a single identity.

But Burt came from a different entertainment area. He was a movie star with a work schedule far different from hers.

He once asked her a strange question: "Would you marry me?"

Not "will" you, but "would" you.

She said, "No."

"Why not?"

"I would never want to be Mrs. Burt Reynolds," she told him. "I have my own identity, and you would never want to be the husband of Tammy Wynette. It wouldn't work. I don't want to share my mirror with anybody."

I also think she felt that Burt was not exactly husband material. He had a jet-set lifestyle, was surrounded by adoring women and seemed to love every minute of it.

"If I walked down the aisle with him," Mom once joked, "he would probably stop and flirt with every pretty girl in the church."

No, Burt wouldn't stay in the picture long, but Mom was restless for another permanent relationship. Dating was unsatisfactory to her. She wanted a husband.

While our house on Franklin Road was being repaired, we lived in an apartment for about three months, and during that time, Mom had a couple of dates with Michael Tomlin, who was in the real estate business and a rakish man-about-town. He drove expensive cars, lived in an expensive apartment and wined and dined Mom in the most expensive restaurants.

It wasn't money, or the appearance of it, that turned Mom's head—she had plenty of money of her own. Partly, it was that he moved in a different social sphere populated by young, energetic, educated, successful, well-dressed, politically connected deal-makers—different enough from the rough-hewn country-music crowd to tantalize her.

On their third date, he proposed. Mom, being reasonable for a change, declined. She didn't love him, she would later admit; and besides, she was still carrying a torch for Burt Reynolds.

She and Sheila Richey went down to Florida to start fixing up the beach house, and, no doubt, Mom carried with her hopes of seeing Burt down there. He was nowhere around and Mom became lonely (a dangerous emotion for her) and a little insecure (a more dangerous emotion for her).

They had only been there a day or two when Mom, thinking about Burt and the impossibility of that relationship, made another of her rueful decisions.

"Sheila, I'm going to marry Michael Tomlin," she blurted out to her astonished friend.

She called her mother to tell her the news. MeeMaw was shocked enough to suggest they talk about this step before Mom actually took it. No deal. Her mind was made up.

She came back to Nashville, collected her daughters and moved us down to Jupiter, saying nothing about her plans to marry again. We found out about it when reporters from *The National Enquirer* came to the house asking questions about her romance with Burt Reynolds.

She tried to deny there was anything between them, but the reporters persisted and pointed to her purchase of the Jupiter house, so close to his ranch, as evidence to the contrary.

"Won't this make it more convenient for you to see Burt?" one reporter asked.

"No," Mom said, "because I'm getting married."

The reporters were speechless. Gwen and I were speechless.

When they were gone, Mom talked to us for a while, told us about Michael and how much she liked being with him and how he could be the strength and stability she had been searching for. She didn't talk at all about love.

A LOT OF people around Mom had serious reservations about her pending marriage, but none could reason with her. George Jones tried to get her to reconsider, but she told him to butt out.

Her mother and stepfather made no attempt to conceal their silent disapproval, but she paid them no mind.

John Lentz, her lawyer, tried to persuade her to sign a prenuptial agreement with her fiancé for her own protection. Michael Tomlin may have appeared to be financially secure but, Lentz argued, safeguards are always wise.

She wouldn't even consider it. She told John that she loved Michael and this marriage would last. "It's real this time," she insisted.

Would she ever learn? Why was having a husband so important that she would deceive herself time and again? Why would she gamble that love would grow from soil she knew to be barren? And, she knew this turf was infertile.

The night before she was to be married, the rhythm guitar player, Charlie Carter, went to her bus and found her crying.

"Do you love this Michael?" he asked her. "If you don't, it's not too late to back out of this."

She didn't tell him that she didn't love Michael, she just said, "I couldn't call this wedding off now anyway. It's tomorrow. I couldn't do that to Michael."

We were still living in our apartment, but the wedding was to take place at the big house on Franklin Road. The backyard had been transformed into a floral garden and the caterer had turned the pool area, where the reception would be, into a colorful splash of tropical fruit and a five-tiered wedding cake.

This was Mom's fourth marriage, but it was her first real wedding. All the others had been hurried civil rites in out-of-the-way places with no friends or relatives present. Finally, she was going to have a complete ceremony, with pastel attendants and tuxedoed groomsmen and live music.

George Richey played piano and his wife, Sheila, was matron of honor.

I wanted to be happy for her, but it seemed too hasty, too staged, too superficial. Michael was a stranger to me, and Mom didn't know him much better. It was almost like the wedding was taking place on a movie set and when it was over, the director would yell, "Cut!" and the actors would go their separate ways.

Mom's friends wanted to be happy for her, too, but without exception, they believed she was making another mistake. Nan Crafton, who had fixed her hair for the ceremony, followed her around all morning, saying over and over, "It's not too late."

For Tammy Wynette it was. Later, she would admit that she wanted to bolt and run, but couldn't, not even when Nan tried to persuade her to make a getaway on a golf cart.

She couldn't embarrass Michael. She couldn't let her friends and her family know that she knew this was a mistake. To her, it was another rock in the cotton sack: Maybe it will work. Maybe . . .

Ten

ALL THE BAD vibes before the wedding proved to be omens of pinpoint accuracy. Nothing, as far as I could ever determine, went right. It was obvious from the beginning that Mr. and Mrs. Tomlin were of such disparate personalities, backgrounds and styles that logging chains would not be able to hold them together. But the first assault on the marriage was of neither's making.

The day after the wedding, Mom and Michael left for Washington, D.C., where she was to perform at the White House for President and Mrs. Gerald Ford and a lot of foreign dignitaries. From there, they were going to Hawaii for their honeymoon.

But by the time she got to the White House that afternoon to rehearse with her band, Mom was experiencing severe abdominal pains, which she dealt with in the way to which she had become accustomed: pills. That got her through the evening's performance, but the pains persisted in Hawaii, where they became so intense she had to be hospitalized and again treated with painkillers.

When they got back to Nashville, she was still hurting but refused to see her doctor for fear that he would insist on operating on her. She had no time for that. She and Michael planned to be in town only for a couple of days before going to Florida on her bus, along with about a dozen friends Michael had invited, to spend a week at the beach house.

They were in Nashville such a short time that my sisters and I had no opportunity to get acquainted with our mother's new husband. Now I realize that is an insignificant point. What really mattered was that Mom had not had much chance to get to know him, either.

At the beach house, they apparently did not spend much time alone. Michael and his friends partied hard and late every night and Mom spent most of her time cooking and grocery shopping and entertaining the crowd. When they returned to Nashville, she looked tired and drawn. I didn't know then about her pain and the steady flow of medication that had sustained her since the wedding, but I knew something was wrong.

A couple of days later, her stomachache became unbearable and she was forced to see her doctor. He examined her, scheduled gallbladder surgery for the next morning and sent her straight to the hospital. She spent the night there alone. Her husband visited the next day, after she had been operated on.

She stayed in the hospital for eight days, and when she was released, she wanted to go back to Florida to rest. Michael invited another couple to go along and I went, too, with one of my girlfriends.

During that time, I still didn't really get to know

Michael very well. He was handsome and charming, but sort of distant. I had the sense that Mom was almost an outsider to his group. She was still weak from the surgery and in no mood to party with them.

One night, Mom had gone to bed early and my friend and I were in the living room watching television. Michael and his friends were somewhere outside.

Suddenly, we heard shouting down on the beach and then gunshots. We were scared stiff, but we looked outside and saw Michael and his friends on the beach. Mom had been awakened by the noise and came tottering into the living room.

"What is going on?" she asked. She was groggy and her eyes were swollen.

"Michael's lost it," I shouted. "He's down on the beach shooting a gun."

She went outside to confront and disarm him.

I don't know exactly what happened later that night, but Mom told me that when they were alone in the bedroom, she and Michael came to a consensus: the marriage wasn't working out. The next morning, he and his friends flew back to Nashville. Mom, my friend and I headed back the following day, but we got only as far as Atlanta, where we had a layover and change of planes.

While we were killing time in the airport, Mom became nauseated and nearly passed out. We took her into the bathroom, where she could splash water on her face, and examined the incision from her gallbladder surgery. Instead of healing, it had become infected and swollen and was oozing pus.

"I don't think I can make it home," she told me. She could barely walk back to the waiting area, and once there, she could barely sit up.

She knew that Burt Reynolds was in Atlanta making the movie *Smokey and the Bandit,* which had been filming since before she married Michael. Therefore, she knew where he was staying. She said she wanted to call him to see if he could recommend a doctor in Atlanta. She was seriously ailing, but I think she wanted to see Burt as much as she wanted to see a doctor.

Burt wasn't at the hotel, but a woman who worked there offered to find Mom a doctor if she would come to the hotel. It was an agonizing cab ride, and after we had checked in, the wait for the doctor seemed interminable.

When he finally arrived, he took one look at Mom's incision and said, "You have a serious infection."

"I guessed that," Mom said.

"We have to get you to the hospital right away," he said. Mom balked.

"Can you just give me something for the pain so I can get back to Nashville in the morning? My regular doctor is there," she said.

The doctor continued to examine the inflamed incision and shook his head.

"That's not a good idea," he said.

"I've got my daughter and her friend with me," Mom argued. "I need to get them home. Isn't there something you can do to get me by until morning?"

He relented, but very reluctantly. He gave her painkillers and antibiotics and left, promising to return early the next morning.

Burt also came by when he had finished shooting for the day and I was thrilled to see him. He had given me a pony several weeks earlier and I hugged him and thanked him for the gift. He was as sweet as always, but not his usual funny self. He seemed impatient to talk to Mom, so I left the room.

They talked for only a short time, and when Burt came out of the bedroom and walked past me, there were tears in his eyes.

The next morning, the doctor returned, and this time he was adamant about getting Mom to the hospital. The infection had worsened and, he told her, she was in no shape to fly to Nashville. Instead, he called an ambulance.

She was in the hospital for five days before the doctors could bring the infection under control. Burt came by a few times and his sister visited a lot. Mom was always more vibrant when Burt was around, but at the same time, I think his presence frightened her. He resurrected feelings she thought, or hoped, she had excised, I believe. Her feelings for him—rather, the knowledge that those feelings were futile—had driven her to Michael Tomlin in the beginning, and now they were doing it again.

As we were checking her out of the hospital, she handed me yet another surprise.

"Maybe I should call Michael and apologize to him," she said. "I don't think that what happened was my fault, but maybe it would be the best thing to do."

As young as I was, I knew they were a misfit and I suspected that Michael was not everything Mom thought he was. Not only had she paid for the wedding, which cost more than $15,000, but while she was in the hospital for gallbladder surgery, Michael went to Mom's bank and told them he wanted to borrow $8,000, using the explanation that he needed it to pay her hospital bill. The need was doubtful, since Mom's insurance policy paid for everything.

At that moment, though, she seemed completely lost and willing to do anything to anchor her life again. She wanted my endorsement and I couldn't deny her that.

"Go ahead," I said. "At least you will know that you've done your best."

She called Michael and apologized for the bad way the marriage had started and asked if he would pick us up at the airport. When she got off the phone, she was smiling and optimistic again.

"He'll be there," she said.

He wasn't. Michael had called Gwen and asked her to meet us.

That was the last effort Mom made to salvage the sunken ship. She filed for an annulment. The summer of 1976 was strange, indeed. She and Michael had been together forty-four days.

No SOONER HAD we arrived home from Atlanta than Mom's condition turned bad again, and she went back into the hospital—this time for five days, but I suspect that wasn't long enough. She had a work schedule and a crew that depended on her, so she went back on the road, coping with her pain in the only way she knew how. Her dependency on painkillers became chronic during that period of her life. She graduated from pills to injections, mostly Demerol, and the dosages grew increasingly stronger.

But in many ways, that was the beginning of an interesting and fun time in the Tammy Wynette orbit. Her marriage to Michael Tomlin had soured her on men, at least for a little while, and so she surrounded herself with family and girlfriends. She still saw Burt now and then, but what I remember most about that period is that our house became something like a girls' dormitory, one long slumber party.

It was during that time that Mom was persuaded to write her autobiography and Joan Dew, a writer, moved to town from Los Angeles to collaborate on the book.

Joan stayed at the house briefly but soon rented an apartment for herself and her son, who was about Georgette's age. In fact, she enrolled him in the St. Paul Christian Academy, the same school that Georgette and Tina attended. Even after she moved out, Joan was around a lot, as were Nan Crafton and Jan Smith and several other friends. They went on shopping trips together and had long lunches and dinners, and, as always, Mom loved cooking for all of them.

For me, it was a pleasant departure from the tension and turmoil that had accompanied Mom's four marriages. She seemed to enjoy that time, too. She accepted Burt as a friend now, not as a potential spouse, and did not seem eager to hook up with another man.

One day, she told Joan Dew, "I need a retired couple to move into this house. The wife could take care of the inside and the man could take care of the outside."

Joan could easily see why she needed help. The house was huge and had tennis courts, an Olympic-size pool and enough bedrooms to billet a small army. We had a cook and housekeeper, but Mom wanted someone to oversee everything and to tend to her children. Gwen and I were in high school and didn't really need a nanny, but I guess we still needed reliable supervision.

Between Mom's work schedule and her medical problems—in just over a year, she had been hospitalized eight times, undergone three surgeries and fought an ear infection and a growth on her vocal cords—she didn't have time to take care of everything herself.

In trying to find someone, Joan called the St. Paul Christian Academy and talked to the school secretary. Maybe she would know a retired teacher who would want the job. No, the secretary said, but she knew a teacher who would be ideal.

Cathye Leshay taught third grade at the academy and was the cheerleader sponsor. Tina, coincidentally, was one of her cheerleaders. The job interested her. Running the Wynette household would pay better than teaching and, no doubt, would be far more interesting.

"Let's meet," Joan said. "Want to have some coffee?"

Cathye said, "Heck, no. I want to come to the house. I want to see where I'm going to be living."

"Fine," Joan said.

"There's one thing," Cathye said, thinking this might be a deal breaker. "I have a dog. She'll have to come, too."

"No problem," Joan said. "Tammy loves animals."

Mom was away when Cathye came to the house. She and Joan hit it off immediately and Cathye was impressed with the surroundings. The house was large enough that she would have plenty of privacy. More important, she and Tammy's daughters shared an instant mutual affection.

"You're perfect," Joan told her.

My sisters and I couldn't have agreed more. She wasn't like the previous nannies and overseers we had known. She was witty and educated and easygoing. For Georgette and Tina, the younger daughters, she could be invaluable.

Mom flew back to town the next day, met Cathye and hired her on the spot at double her teaching salary. She moved in at the end of the week, but she brought along only her clothes. Everything else she left in her apartment, which she had decided to keep until she knew how this job would work out.

It worked out wonderfully. Cathye gave stability to a home that had seen its share of turbulence. She tutored Georgette and Tina and became a trusted counselor to Gwen and me. We could talk to her about clothes, boyfriends, our plans for the future, anything, and if her advice was not required, she was always a sympathetic ear.

She also fit beautifully into the female sorority.

With her exhausting work agenda and her recurring health problems, you would have thought that on her days off Mom would have collapsed into bed and stayed there as long as she could. She would have been better off doing that once in a while, but she pushed herself to live as well as work. At times, she seemed almost manic, coming in on the bus at midnight and getting up early the next morning with a road trip on her mind.

"I'm bored. Let's go someplace," she would say to who-ever was around. They would rush down to Jupiter for a few days on the beach, or head to Mississippi or Alabama to visit relatives or old friends, or jump on a plane to visit some club where James Hollie, her bass player and band manager, was working.

She had a compulsion to be constantly on the go, no matter what the conditions. One night, a snowstorm had closed most of the roads in Nashville, but she was deter-mined to get away.

"We're going skiing," she told us.

Jan Smith was at the house that day with her son, Can-non, who is the same age as Georgette. We all piled into the white limousine and set out for Gatlinburg, two hun-dred miles away, in the Great Smoky Mountains. We slipped and slid halfway across the state before Mom stopped at some little backwoods gas station and had chains put on the limo. We had a ball on that trip. Sometimes we would jump on a plane for Colorado or California or anywhere her whims dictated. There weren't many dull moments back then.

Spontaneous travel had always been in Mom's nature, and those impromptu journeys certainly kept her friends entertained.

She and Jan went to Florida once and stopped at a small bar somewhere near Lakeland. Throughout the trip, Mom kept insisting that she did not want to be recognized. She wanted to relax and not be fussed over by fans. But when they got inside the bar, there was a small band playing, and it was pretty good.

"I want to sing with this band," Mom told Jan.

"Fine," Jan sighed, "but they're going to recognize you."

Mom talked to the band and even though they didn't know her from Lizzie Borden, they agreed to let her sing. She did two numbers, "Help Me Make It Through the Night" and "Satin Sheets"—neither one a Tammy Wynette song.

On the way back to her table, she passed an old woman sitting at the bar. She was a little loaded and, by Jan's description, looked as though she had been roosting on that stool for three weeks.

"Honey," the woman said when Mom walked by, "you ought to go to Nashville. I think you could make it there."

"Thank you so much," Mom said. "A lot of people have told me that."

"You ain't bad," the woman said.

She and Jan laughed for weeks about that.

* * *

MAYBE I'M INSERTING too much retrospection into my memories of that period after her breakup with Michael Tomlin, but I think some of Mom's compulsive gallivanting was not so much a pursuit of amusement as it was an escape from the void that always consumed her when there was no man in her life.

Certainly, she had suitors during that time. Burt was still in the picture, at least until early 1977, and I know she dated a few other men and, as always, George Richey was around an awful lot. I didn't think much about it then. He was still married to Sheila, who was one of Mom's dear friends, and my sisters and I thought of Richey and Sheila the same way, as family friends.

His feelings for Mom may have had something to do with his separation from Sheila, and if that is the case, he almost cast his lot with a lost cause.

It was sometime around the end of 1977 when Richey stopped by the studio, where Mom was recording. He wasn't there to help with her music. Rather, he wanted to tell her that he and Sheila were getting a divorce. My guess is that he hoped that the news would draw her to him. What he may not have known, though, was that Mom was pretty heavily involved with someone else, someone she thought she wanted to marry.

Her new flame was a celebrity, too, a well-known country singer. And, he was very married.

Eleven

EVEN IF TAMMY Wynette's daughters and friends and associates had known everything that we know now, it is doubtful that we could have influenced her decision.

We still don't know a lot about George Richey before he came to Nashville in 1968. I now know that he was born George Richardson in Arkansas, in a place called Promise Land, in 1934, and that he married Dorothy Ann Tippitt when he was nineteen.

When they moved to Nashville from Memphis, they had two children, a daughter, Deirdre, and a son, Kelly. He was only thirty-three, but going by the name George Richey, he became established pretty quickly as a musician, songwriter and producer and, in general, a musical wizard. Whether he was working with a small country band of self-taught musicians who didn't even read music, or a full-blown symphony, everyone said, he was a master of his art.

You have to be pretty good to make it in Nashville, as a

couple of million wannabes can testify. A river of hopeful young men and women flows down Music Row every year—writers, pickers, singers—all convinced they are big-time-bound, only to learn the gory truth: the town is a graveyard of broken hearts and broken dreams.

To a lot of people, country music looks simple. A twang, a lament, three chords and the truth. Behind the hats and the rhinestones and the honky-tonks, though, is a complex, sophisticated and demanding business. Pure talent will get you inside, but it takes cunning and instinct and intensity to keep you there. Richey had all of those assets.

He also developed a reputation for an explosive temper and an abusive tongue.

In 1975, he was producing various artists for Capitol Records. One day Charlie Louvin showed up for a recording session, which got off to a slow start because, Louvin noticed, Richey was distracted by a young woman hanging around the sound control room with her poodle. As time passed, Louvin became impatient and then angry. He was paying for the studio time and Richey's dawdling was costing him money. Richey had not given him and his band any musical arrangements, so they began working on their own.

Richey heard their impromptu rehearsal and burst into the studio.

"I want to know who the son-of-a-bitch was who changed my arrangements," he shouted.

"You didn't give us any arrangements," Charlie said.

"This is my goddamn session," Richey ranted. "It's my goddamn session."

After a few minutes of listening to his tirade, Charlie said, "Well, since it's your session, you do the singing. I'm out of here."

That same day, Charlie called Capitol's headquarters in Los Angeles and talked to one of the executives.

"Is there someone else I can record with?" he asked.

"Ummm . . . no," the exec said. "Richey is the A and R [in charge of artists and repertoire] in Nashville."

"In that case," Charlie said, "you can send my contract back to me."

He left Capitol and signed with United Artists.

Some of that temperament also surfaced in Richey's personal life. Nashville may have been no harder on his marriage than it is on everyone else's in the music business, but the circuit-court records of Davidson County do not paint a flattering portrait of him.

It's only her version, of course, but when Dorothy sued him for divorce in the late 1960s, a year after they arrived in Nashville, she alleged:

> *Soon after the separation, defendant told complainant that it was embarrassing to him to have a wife and children living in Nashville and he insisted that [she] and the children move to Memphis.*
>
> *On or about October 20, 1969, defendant told complainant that he wanted a divorce from her and that he had a lawyer who would get him a divorce in Arizona and he insisted that [she] sign papers which his lawyer had prepared. When complainant refused to sign the papers, which contained an agreement that [she] would receive a grossly inadequate amount of money for alimony and child support, [he] became angry and has tried on numerous occasions since then to force her to sign said papers against her will.*

By Nashville standards—especially compared to my mother's marital debacles—that is pretty tepid stuff, but it makes an important point. After one year in town, Richey, who was driving a new Cadillac and running with the music-industry players, had distanced himself from the relative drabness of home and family.

It was his second divorce that, had we known the details then, would have sent up red flags.

He married Sheila Hall in 1974, and a year later she was at the courthouse with a divorce petition. However, the papers reflect that a reconciliation took place and they didn't actually divorce until 1978. Allegations made by Sheila in both the 1975 petition that was dismissed when they reconciled and Sheila's 1978 divorce complaint, along with restraining orders issued against Richey in connection with the divorce proceedings, suggest a disturbing side of him.

On their first anniversary, she charged, they went to a restaurant and at some point during the evening Richey became angry with her. She alleged:

> *Upon [their] arrival at their home [he] proceeded to physically beat her and physically abuse her, removed her keys to the home, took her pocketbook away from her, drug her to a door, carrying off her clothes and rendering her partially nude and bodily threw her out of the home, whereupon plaintiff was required to walk through dense woods and through neighbors' yards to the home of a friend, where she spent the night. Plaintiff avers that she is dreadfully afraid of the defendant.*
>
> *Plaintiff will show that the defendant has previously rendered physical abuse to her, specifically on*

> *December 12, 1974, when he refused to let her leave*
> *the home and proceeded to burn clothing in the mid-*
> *dle of the floor in their house.*
>
> *Plaintiff will show that on one previous occasion*
> *in March that the defendant violently physically*
> *abused her, as well as on many previous occasions.*

Dragging his wife. Shoving her out of the house nearly naked. Setting fire to her clothes in the house. If those allegations were true, that is a disturbing sketch of a cold, tyrannical and dangerous person. When a property settlement was struck between Sheila and Richey, the divorce was ultimately granted on the grounds of "irreconcilable differences" and all other grounds were officially stricken from the complaint, so the court never determined whether these allegations were true.

Even if we had known about those charges, though, we probably could not have precluded the inevitable.

I'M NOT GOING to identify the married man with whom Mom was involved. That was a long time ago, and it would serve no purpose to embarrass him or to create problems for him now. As far as I know, he is still married and, I hope, happily so.

He is important to this narrative only because he was, like Burt Reynolds, important enough to Mom to muddle her thinking and send her retreating into another marriage for the wrong reason.

While that affair was ongoing, Richey was becoming an important part of her professional life. He helped her with her musical arrangements, wrote songs for her and sometimes sat in with her band when her piano player was ill. And he pursued her with a passion.

Once again, she found herself in that familiar and distracting position of being in love with one man while another was begging her to marry him. Her friends have told me that she truly believed that her lover was going to divorce his wife. When he declined to do that, she rebounded to Richey the same way she had rebounded to Michael Tomlin.

Even so, I think, everyone, with a few exceptions, was pleased that this time the one who caught her was Richey. He and Mom seemed to have a lot in common and he was a tireless worker, a deft organizer and a consummate guardian and protector—the qualities Mom had always sought in a husband. Outwardly, he was accommodating almost to the point of fawning in the presence of Tammy Wynette. She had only to hint of a need or a want and Richey was there.

It was probably in the late winter or early spring of 1978 when Richey moved into the house, set up an office and began to assume most of the duties of managing Tammy Wynette. They were making wedding plans.

Cathye Leshay had been living there for five or six months when Richey called her to his office.

"Cathye, we just adore you, but Tammy and I are in love and we want to spend the rest of our lives together," he said.

Cathye nodded her approval.

"We need it to be just the two of us," Richey went on.

"Absolutely," she said. "I don't blame you one bit."

"I've got to get rid of all these females around her," Richey said. "Do you understand?"

"Sure," she said.

"Don't get me wrong, honey. You've done a great job, but I've just got to let it be family. I hope you understand."

"Absolutely," Cathye said. "When do you want me to leave?"

"Just whenever it's convenient," he said.

Because Cathye had kept her apartment, she was able to pack her clothes and be out in a couple of days. It didn't take much longer than that for her to find another teaching job.

The sorority was disbanded and Mom's girlfriends came around less and less. Nan Crafton, who had been Mom's hairdresser for years, was not invited to find work elsewhere—not yet—but she contemplated quitting for reasons of her own.

"I'm getting out," she told her sister, Jan. "I can't stick around and condone this marriage."

She had an ominous feeling about Richey. She felt that in subtle ways he began to manipulate Mom and everyone around her and tried to isolate her from everyone who had been close to her. She didn't carry through then with her threat to quit her job, but as time passed, her negative perceptions of Richey continued.

Richey's family began to move into the house. Paul and Sylvia Richardson moved in first. His mother and father, who lived in Malden, Missouri, came later, and Deirdre and Kelly were there just about every holiday. By summer, the house was overflowing with Richardsons, some of whom were on Mom's payroll—and this was months before she and Richey were married.

Work on Mom's autobiography was still ongoing that spring, so Joan Dew was one of the regulars that Richey could not send packing. But he tried, and that may have been the first clue that the rest of us had to his controlling and manipulative nature.

Like everyone else, Joan was concerned about Mom's drug addiction. When she first arrived on the scene, Mom was taking Demerol orally but sporadically, sometimes going a week or two without it. Over a year's or year and a half's period, Joan saw the frequency and the dosages increase. Sometimes, she noticed, Mom would take 100 milligrams of Demerol by injection and another 50 milligrams orally—enough to knock out a large man for surgery—and then do a full show.

Joan even did some research on the drug. Essentially it is a synthetic opiate with pharmacologic properties similar to morphine, but its effects do not last as long. Medical texts say it will produce both psychologic and physical dependence and an overdose will cause severe respiratory depression. Some of the side effects are transient hallucinations, hypotension, visual disturbances, confusion, convulsions, dizziness, drowsiness and slow heartbeat.

Obviously, it is not something you want to see a friend or loved one using for an extended period of time. Some nurses told Joan that many doctors would prescribe morphine instead of Demerol because morphine is less addictive. Demerol, in fact, is more addictive than heroin or cocaine, they told her, and addicts will go to great lengths to get the drug, even injuring themselves, if necessary, in the process.

Doctors are often too accommodating to celebrities, but even Tammy Wynette couldn't just walk into a doctor's office in a strange city, ask for a fix and be assured of getting one. She had to have a ruse and she would go to extremes to create one.

Once, playing an outdoor show at a fair somewhere in the West, Mom fell off the stage and injured her elbow. At least I thought that was what had happened. Joan told me the truth much later.

"She pretended to faint," Joan said, "and *threw herself* off the stage. It wasn't an accident. She had to knock Nan and me out of the way to do it."

That stunt was good for a few months of Demerol. At every stop after that, she would find a doctor who was willing to give her a prescription for the pain, caused by a damaged nerve, in her elbow. A few months later, she had surgery to correct it.

Another time, she was playing the El Fiesta Club in Seguin, Texas, when she complained of stomach pains. A helicopter took her to the county hospital in San Antonio, but she left the emergency room before the physicians had time to complete their examination. Her explanation to reporters was that she disagreed with their diagnosis.

In fact, they had not rendered one when she left in a huff. Mom demanded painkillers, but the doctors would not comply until they had determined what was wrong with her. Administering painkillers too early, they explained to her, makes it difficult to determine where the pain is. Mom stormed out of the emergency room with the doctors pleading with her to let them complete the examination.

Because of incidents like those, Joan Dew came to the conclusion that Mom had a serious drug addiction. She discussed it often with Nan and Jan, and the three of them tried to talk to Richey about it. Hoping that he would try to help Mom beat her addiction, they bought a *Physicians' Desk Reference,* a book that had information on just about every drug on the market, and showed Richey what Mom was taking. They wanted him to understand the nature of the drug, its addictive potency and the consequences of its abuse.

Rather than heed the warnings, Richey used their "meddling" to try to turn Mom against them. He told Mom that Joan was spreading rumors all over Nashville that she was a drug addict. Joan said she had discussed it with no one but Jan and Nan.

Despite her negative feelings about him, Nan had nonetheless been hopeful that Richey would be Mom's savior. But, it didn't turn out that way at all.

Nan was horrified one day when Mom was apparently suffering withdrawal and Richey injected her with Demerol, giving her the assurance, "As long as you're with me, you'll never want. . . ."

Years later, Nan told me she knew at that moment that this marriage would bring no salvation to Tammy Wynette.

THE WEDDING TOOK place on an incandescent day on the beach fifty yards behind the house in Jupiter. Beside a stand of sea grape brush, striped awnings were set up to shelter the guests from the July sun. A small group of spectators, held back by a police boundary, watched from a short distance away. A few photographers had hired boats to get them close enough to spy on the ceremony. Photos of Tammy Wynette's wedding were worth something to the tabloids. There was little commotion, though, and security was not a big problem.

Strangely enough, the wedding was of little interest to Nashville. Recently, I found an old newspaper clipping that opened my eyes to how Mom's friends, and her industry cohorts, viewed her marriage to Richey. It reported that even though police were told to expect all the top country-western singers and hired thirty off-duty officers to augment their small force, the stars did not show up. Said Stanley Shiffert, police chief of Florida's Jupiter Inlet Colony, "Imagine my horror and embarrassment when no stars showed up. There was no one to protect. I hope that was her last wedding."

WAS NASHVILLE JUST getting weary of Tammy Wynette's forays into matrimony, or was there something else that kept everyone away? It had all the makings of an exuberant, sun-splashed shindig. Richey's father, the Reverend C. R. Richardson, performed the ceremony. Mom's parents were there, and PeePaw would walk her down the aisle once again. Mom's aunt Carolyn, whom she had always considered a sister, was dying of cancer but managed to make it to Florida that day. The Statesmen, Mom's favorite gospel quartet, were there to serenade her.

It turns out that for Mom, the day was anything but festive.

Before the ceremony, she was in the bathroom, touching up her hair. Joan Dew walked in and found her nearly in tears.

"Are you okay?" she asked.

Mom nodded.

Joan knew what was wrong.

"Tammy, you don't have to do this," she said.

"Yes I do," Mom said.

"Please don't do this," she said. "You know you're not in love with this man."

Mom looked at her with sad eyes and a long face, but

said nothing. She looked like someone about to go into surgery rather than to the altar, Joan would later recall.

"I've seen you in love and this is not it," Joan pleaded.

"I don't have a choice," Mom said. "It's too late."

"Tammy, it's never too late."

"Yes, it is. It's too late for me."

Mom was straight and sober and lucid then, but later, when it was time for the ceremony, she was so looped on Demerol that her stepfather practically had to carry her down the aisle.

Twelve

YOU WOULD THINK that if someone in your family was kidnapped, beaten and dumped along a rural roadside eighty miles from home, it would be a big topic of conversation around the house. Yet when that supposedly happened to my mother, the subject was almost taboo. Everyone in the family was petrified, especially since it followed so closely the string of death threats, harassing phone calls, intrusions, vandalism and fires that had disrupted our lives for nearly a year.

Those incidents had ceased about a year and a half earlier, but now, just three months after her marriage to Richey, we had reason to believe that the terrorism was back—and more menacing. Someone had snatched my mother from a crowded parking lot and held her captive for two hours!

In most families, I assume, that would be the stuff of long and searching discussions in which the who's and the why's and the what-if's were sifted through. If Tammy

Wynette was at risk, were her children safe? Would the house become a target again? Who had a motive to terrorize us? What precautions should we take?

Instead, it was something we didn't talk about. About the only details I knew of the incident were those I learned from the newspapers. Whenever I asked Mom about it, she would dismiss the subject by saying, "That's all over now."

At the time it happened, I was only sixteen and not wise enough to see behind her reticence. Living with Tammy Wynette was not a normal existence, and this was just another abnormality, one that wasn't discussed.

Besides, Mom and Richey had only been married about three months and the household was a little chaotic anyway, what with Mom's four daughters and Richey's son and daughter trying to adjust to each other. So the events of October 4, 1978, were treated like some ugly beast that had strayed into the house and was quickly locked up in the cellar.

Years later, I would learn from my mother's lips a different version of the story, but at the time all anyone knew was what was laid out in police reports and newspaper articles. This is what the world was being told:

Mom said she had gone to the Green Hills Mall on a Wednesday afternoon to drop some jewelry off to be cleaned and to do some shopping for Georgette. She went into a couple of stores and then left her jewelry at E. J. Sain about a quarter past five o'clock.

When she got back to her car, which she said she had left unlocked, a man wearing part of a tan stocking or some kind of mesh over his face was hiding in the backseat. She told the police that he put a gun to her back, forced her to get behind the wheel and said, "Drive."

That, by her account, was the only word he said directly

to her for the next two hours. By gesturing with the pistol in his hand, he directed her to drive out Hillsboro Road. Just before they reached Franklin Road, he directed her to stop and get in the backseat and on the floorboard. He then got out of the car, and Mom could hear him talking to another man, she said.

The abductor then returned to the car and ordered Mom to get back behind the wheel. They drove south on Interstate 65 at normal speed for about an hour and turned off on a state highway, where he signaled her to stop again, she said, somewhere near Pulaski, just north of the Alabama line.

As he forced her out of the car, she said, she asked him over and over, "What do you want from me?"

She said he wrapped a piece of panty hose around her neck and slammed his fist into her head, not hard enough to knock her out but enough to stun her. She said she saw a blue station wagon drive up. Her kidnapper got in and the two men drove away, she said.

That part was her story. The rest is a matter of record, backed up by witnesses.

Though her car was still there, she stumbled away and was spotted about seven-thirty by Bobby Young, who was pulling out of the driveway of his family's farmhouse. She collapsed beside the road and told Young, "I need help."

Young and his mother took her into their house. They removed the stocking that was wrapped around her neck and told her to lie on the sofa. They brought wet towels to clean her swollen and bloody lips and the bruise left by the assailant's fist.

"He tried to kill me. He tried to kill me," Mom kept saying.

They called the Giles County Sheriff's Department and a couple of deputies took Mom to the hospital. Word of the incident had gotten around and reporters were calling. The doctors told them that Mom would be admitted to stay overnight.

At ten-thirty, though, Richey arrived and whisked her out a side door and into his car.

It soon became obvious to just about everyone who read the news accounts that this was a very strange crime. She wasn't raped. She wasn't robbed. There was no demand for ransom. By Mom's account, she was snatched from a shopping-mall parking lot, driven sixty or seventy miles away and punched in the head for no good reason. Why would she have left her car, containing packages she had purchased that day, unlocked? Why would kidnappers take her away in her car, a flashy yellow Cadillac that was easily recognized, instead of their own car?

THE GRAPEVINES AND phone lines of Music Row were buzzing almost immediately, and unfortunately, most of the speculation was about George Jones. The newspapers had pointed out that although they had divorced more than three years earlier, there was still hostility between them— specifically, child-support hostility.

While it is true that Mom had gone to court to collect $36,000 she believed that he owed her, I felt the suspicions about Jones were misplaced.

But in trying to make sense of the mystery, the police developed a theory that centered on Jones, or someone in his organization. He had an alibi—he was at his home in Florence, Alabama—but that would not have prevented him from hiring someone to do the job, the police reasoned. Or someone close to him could have acted independently.

Jones had just recorded an album and the judge had ordered that some of the proceeds be impounded to pay his child-support debt. The official suspicion was that some of Jones's managers could have staged the kidnapping to scare Mom off so they could retain control of Jones's money.

Whatever the facts of the child-support payments were, there was one fact of which I was certain: George Jones would never hurt my mother, especially over something as inconsequential to him as money. On a drinking binge, Jones could be volatile, but a cold-blooded, premeditated assault on my mother is something that would have to be conceived and executed with some degree of sobriety. Jones had been nothing but kind and loving to my sisters and me, and we did not think for a minute that he was capable of such a thing.

If it was a genuine kidnapping, someone other than Jones, I had no doubt, was behind it.

There were other hypotheses floating around. One was that Mom had faked the kidnapping herself to try to revive a slumping career. After virtually owning the Country Music Association's Female Vocalist of the Year Award, she was getting tougher competition from younger singers breaking into the business. That year, someone else—I think Crystal Gayle—won it.

A different version of that same theme had it that Mom really was an innocent victim and that Richey planned the whole thing for publicity.

The police asked Mom to take a lie detector test and she refused. In fact, she wasn't particularly eager to cooperate with the police. When investigators came to the house to talk to her, she would keep them waiting for an hour or longer, and when she finally talked to them, she didn't add anything to what she told the deputies the night of the incident.

Richey took a polygraph and apparently passed it, according to Red Smotherman, the Nashville officer who investigated the incident. The examiner said he showed no deception in denying that he knew who kidnapped his wife and in denying that it was a publicity stunt.

I think the police, who were getting nowhere fast, began to suspect it was all some kind of hoax and not really worth their time to investigate.

Mom and Richey hired extra security guards for the house, but about a month after the incident another strange thing happened. A note was placed in the iron gates that protected the driveway:

We missed you the first time. We'll get you the second time.

With a horde of cops and security people patrolling the grounds, how did someone manage to place the note there without being detected? There were no fingerprints on the note, just as there had been none, except for hers, in Mom's car after the kidnapping. What purpose did it serve? Was someone still trying to scare her? Was it another publicity ploy?

Mom seemed to want to put it out of her mind. Everyone else in Nashville, though, loved talking about it. It was one of those subjects that people in the industry would resurrect from time to time when there was nothing better to talk about. As long as it was an unsolved mystery, it would be the stuff of speculation.

* * *

MOM WAS PERFORMING again two days after the incident, and everywhere she went, reporters wanted to question her about it. Her answers were usually brief, the kinds of reflections you would expect from someone who had been terrorized.

"It makes me feel uncomfortable to realize that whoever did it is still out there somewhere," she said in one interview.

As often as he could, Richey tried to intercept the reporters. They were in Las Vegas early in December and a reporter called their hotel room and asked to speak with Mom. Richey declined to put her on the line.

There had been a possible development in the kidnapping investigation, the reporter said, and he would like to ask her about it.

"She's talked about it so much, that's the last thing she'd want to do," Richey said.

The "development" was a confession by a man who said he and an accomplice had been paid $400 to carry out the kidnapping.

The man's name was Buddy Earl Justice and he was in jail on murder charges in Pulaski, Virginia. He bragged to a cellmate named Calvin Crisp that he and Dale D. Goins had gone on a crime spree through the United States and Canada, killing thirty people along the way.

Crisp reported it to the police in Paluski and they passed it along to the FBI, which passed it along to the Nashville detectives investigating the kidnapping.

Nothing ever came of it. Eventually, I believe, the police determined that Justice was, in fact, somewhere else when the kidnapping took place.

So, the gossip droned on. George Jones, or someone associated with him, was behind it. George Richey, or someone associated with him, was behind it. Tammy Wynette staged the whole thing. The police were the only ones in town who had lost interest in the matter.

I always believed that Mom didn't talk about it because there was nothing to say. It happened, it was over, and that was that.

Then, two years later, she gave a long interview to *Penthouse* magazine and revealed something I had never heard her express before.

The writer asked if she had felt like "retreating" after the kidnapping.

"No possible way," she said. "I was back on stage two nights after it happened. I'm a firm believer in what's-gonna-happen's-gonna-happen."

Did the police ever find the guilty party? the writer asked.

"No, they didn't," she said. "Though in my mind, I feel I know who was responsible, but I'd prefer to let it be—if it will."

Why?

"To accuse certain people could cause a lot more problems. What I will say is there was more than one person involved. They were people who had approached me about doing some things career-wise—very legitimate things in the business—and I'd said 'no,' and there was reason for them not to like that. What the police do know now is that it was all preplanned. In fact, three people in Nashville said they knew four hours ahead of time that I was going to be kidnapped. Later, security found out that six of our phone lines had been tapped—even the one in the basement. And these people had a place set up in the woods that surround our house where they had built a little seat to sit on, and the phone box was down at the bottom [of the pole] instead of on top. All they had to do was sit there and listen. And they could see right into the house when the curtains weren't pulled. But nothing's happened since then, so I don't really want to pursue it. I just hope that it's all in the past."

It was a chilling revelation: shadowy figures lurking in the woods, listening to our phone conversations, peering into our windows. At the time I had no reason to doubt it. Still, I could not understand why Mom, if she truly believed she knew who was behind it, would be so willing to let them off. Could it have been the same person or persons who had terrorized us a year earlier?

That was not Mom's nature to let something like that slide so easily. In some ways she could be insecure, especially about her career and her place in country music, but in other ways she was anything but timid. I think it would have taken a powerful motive to suppress her instinct to strike back at those responsible.

Many years would pass before I learned the different version I now believe to be true.

I DON'T REMEMBER the exact date—it was in 1991 or 1992—that Mom first told me she wanted to leave Richey.

I came home one day and found her sitting on her suitcase at the end of my driveway and smoking one cigarette after another.

"What are you doing?" I asked.

"We had an argument," she said.

It must have been a big one. Mom had packed her suitcase and called her friend Betty Bernow and asked if she would pick her up. She carried the suitcase out to Franklin Road and sat there for a long time. I still wonder what passing motorists thought about seeing Tammy Wynette sitting on a suitcase beside the road. Her housekeeper drove up and panicked. She tried to talk Mom into going back inside. Instead, Mom got in her car and drove to my house.

"Let's go inside," I said.

For some reason, she hesitated and lit another cigarette.

"Mom, you're welcome to stay here," I said.

"I know," she said. She was extremely agitated and I was trying to think of some way to calm her.

"Have you eaten?" I asked.

She shook her head.

"Come on," I said. I put her suitcase in my car and we drove to a restaurant over by Interstate 65. Along the way, she started ranting about Richey, telling me she wanted to leave him, that she couldn't take his abuse anymore. She said he was a bully who wanted to control everything about her life.

I knew their marriage was not always idyllic—whose is?—and I was all too familiar with Richey's way of manipulating her and her friends and her children. My sisters and I had seen the way he pushed her to work when she didn't feel like it. We had heard arguments between them and had witnessed outbursts, but we had never heard Mom talk about divorcing him. She had never shown anything but an iron resolve to make this marriage last.

Now she was pouring out her heart to me in a way she had never done before.

"I want you to know something else," she said.

I waited while she sat silently, as though trying to decide if she really wanted to say what was on her mind.

"That kidnapping . . ." she said at last.

I had waited twelve or thirteen years for this conversation and didn't want to say anything to spook her back into silence. I said, "Uh-huh?"

"It didn't happen," she said.

It wasn't exactly what I expected. "You weren't kidnapped?"

"No," she said. "It was all made up."

Her expression told me that this was a painful admission for her, but one she was prepared to continue.

"Why?" I asked.

She became quiet and stared out the window, as calm as if she had slipped into a trance. I wasn't going to let it end there.

"Why would you make up something like that? You had bruises where the guy beat you."

"Richey gave me those bruises," she said.

"He hit you?"

She sighed and said, "Yeah," and then told me that they had had a fight and he punched her. After they had calmed down, Richey realized that the marks on her face would be visible for several days, if not weeks, and Mom had shows to do. He came up with the phony kidnapping and beating to explain the bruises. She had driven herself south, to the roadside where she was found, and Richey waited at home to be notified so he could fetch her from the hospital.

I didn't ask about the threatening note that was placed in the gate a few days after the "kidnapping." I didn't have to. If the abduction was a hoax known only to her and Richey, one of them probably planted it.

Later, I learned that she had told a few close friends the same story. I guess she wanted one of her daughters to hear it. It occurred to me that since she had appeared at my house with her suitcase, she had told me the story so I would be sympathetic to her decision to leave Richey.

We ate dinner and drove back to my house. I was expecting her to stay the night, if not longer, but when we got out of the car, she reached for her suitcase and tossed it into her Cadillac.

"What are you doing?" I asked.

She hugged me and said, "I guess I'm going home."

She had begun to appear edgy, even a little frightened. I was certain that her medication was wearing off, her courage dissipating with it. Richey would be angry about her leaving, and she didn't want to provoke him.

Her fear of Richey, it occurred to me then, a dozen years after their marriage, was a cornerstone of their relationship. If Richey had punched her and then hatched a kidnapping plot to cover it up, what else was he capable of?

Gwen and I talked about the purported kidnapping several times over the years, and each time our minds went back to the terror we had endured that year of fires and flooding and vandalism.

Richey had acknowledged that he loved Tammy Wynette from afar during that time, and it was a time when she was sowing her oats with the likes of Rudy Gatlin and Burt Reynolds and Michael Tomlin, while his marriage to Sheila was ending. The words SLUT and WHORE scribbled in lipstick on walls and mirrors certainly gave a clue to the vandal's motive.

Richey knew the layout of our house and had easy access to it. He also knew Tammy Wynette well enough to know that fear would hasten her yearning to have a man, a protector, on the premises. I don't know for sure, but based on what my mother told me about the kidnapping, I can't help but wonder whether Richey was responsible for our year of terror.

Thirteen

EVERYTHING I HAVE related so far about my mother's drug addiction were things I learned after I had married and moved out of her house. In the years that I lived with her, the years when her dependency began, I was not aware of it and neither were my sisters.

When Mom was at home, she seemed more or less normal to us. We were accustomed to her impulses to jump in the car and prowl the countryside. We were accustomed to her moods. When she was tired, that seemed perfectly natural for someone with her work schedule. When she was fired up about something, such as preparing a holiday feast for a dozen or more guests, her tireless energy was not surprising.

Although the household was different after she married Richey, there was nothing in the new routine that raised red flags about excessive use of painkillers. If anything, she seemed happier and more relaxed. Richey, with the help of his family, had taken over management of nearly all of her

LEFT: Here's my mom as a young woman, when her singing career was still just a dream. *(Everett Collection)*

BELOW: One of my mom's earlier publicity stills. Look at all that mascara! *(Photofest)*

ABOVE: Doing what she loved
best. *(Bob Noble/Globe Photos, Inc.)*

RIGHT: Mom's look tended
to flow with the times.
(Globe Photos, Inc.)

BELOW: Mom and me in front
of our house in the early 1970s.
(Gwen Nicholas)

ABOVE: Here she is in a more thoughtful pose.
(Everett Collection)

LEFT: Mom went through a phase of wearing these beaded gowns. They weighed a ton, but she loved them.
(Richard Open/ Camera Press/Retna)

RIGHT: Me, singer Trisha Yearwood and Mom at the Fan Fair Country Music Festival in Nashville.
(Gwen Nicholas)

BELOW: Lee Roy Parnell, Mom, me and my sister Gwen, also at Fan Fair.
(Charles Ignaczak)

Mom with
country great
Johnny Cash . . .
(Everett/CSU Archives)

. . . and with legend
Merle Haggard.
(Beth Gwinn/Retna)

ABOVE: Larry Daly, Mom, Milton Berle and George Richey. *(Martha Dettwiller)*

RIGHT: Mom continued to tour throughout her long career. *(Photofest)*

LEFT: In happier days, George Richey with Mom and her four grandchildren: *(left to right)* my twins, Natalie and Catherine, and Kristina and Sophia. *(George Bodnar/Retna)*

BELOW: At the Rainforest Benefit in 1994, with Whitney Houston, Sting and Luciano Pavarotti. *(Arnaldo Magnani/ Liaison Agency)*

Married or not, my mom and George Jones were always the First Couple of Country Music.

ABOVE: *(Photofest)*

LEFT: *(NBC/Globe Photos)*

BELOW: *(Redferns/Retna)*

business and personal affairs. She welcomed that because, she said at the time, it freed her to concentrate on her music, to write songs and contemplate career moves.

From what I saw, and from what Mom's friends have told me, there appeared to be a genuinely loving side to her relationship with Richey. It was rare that anyone saw them argue, and when they did, it was sometimes more comical than disturbing.

One night, they were alone in the stateroom of the bus but everyone up front could hear their voices rising. Jan Smith was sitting nearest the door and could hear the argument growing louder and louder. Suddenly, the door to the stateroom flew open and Mom yelled, "Jan, call the police and call them now. I want this son-of-a-bitch arrested and I want him off my bus."

Richey glared at Jan and said, "If you touch that telephone, you'll be sorry."

Both Mom and Richey were breathing fire, but the absurdity of it all was so powerful that Jan couldn't hold back the laughter. The only telephone on the bus was an intercom line that connected the stateroom to the driver.

For the most part, at least in the early days of their marriage, they seemed content and compatible. When Mom sang with the Dallas Symphony, Richey was the guest conductor. Once, when she rehearsed for a Las Vegas show with a full orchestra, the sound was awkward. Richey gave everyone a thirty-minute break and wrote a whole new arrangement. He attended to her, catered to her, pampered her, and shielded her—sometimes to excess—from what he considered distracting influences. The problem, as we came to learn, was that he considered her old friends and even her children to be influences from which she needed protection.

But Mom trusted him and admired his organizational abilities nearly as much as his musical talents. He saw to details that had often frustrated or annoyed her, and, in turn, she made him the keeper of her world. His attempts to completely dominate her were only partially successful, though. She stood up to him when she felt the need, and Richey seemed to understand all the lines that should not be crossed.

I ONLY LIVED in their house for two years. Gwen had left home for University of Colorado when I was seventeen, and I departed a year later to marry John Paule, whom I had met in London when I accompanied Mom on one of her European tours. Deirdre and I had gone to a club after Mom's show and John was there with some of his friends.

Originally from Cyprus, John had lived in London for twenty-five years and had a charming, easy manner and casual good looks. I liked him immediately. We stayed in touch after I returned home and he visited a few times. We got married in 1980 on my eighteenth birthday. Mom offered John a job as her road manager and he accepted. We lived in Nashville for the first three years of our marriage and then moved to Florida in 1984. Most of the time, I stayed at home while he traveled with the Tammy Wynette Show.

It was not an unusual arrangement. Very few, if any, of Mom's band members or road crew lived in Nashville. They were scattered around Tennessee, Florida, Texas, Kentucky and God-knows-where-else. When their work-week was finished, they went home. When it was time to hit the road again, they flew into Nashville, rendezvoused at Mom's house and waited for her driver to bring the bus around. The beginning of every trip was like a big party. Mom would usually have big pots of food, which she prepared herself, to feed everyone before the journey.

The first day out, everyone would be fresh and energetic and eager to swap stories or test new songs on each other. Sometimes, with a few hours to kill before a show, they would organize softball games or some other form of diversion. Until the miles and the days started to wear on them, those trips were almost like a family vacation, she often said.

John loved his job as road manager, and he always came home with interesting or amusing stories to tell. But after we had been married a year or two, his mood shifted a little and he seemed stressed or concerned about something.

What had been a big, happy clan was turning into a dysfunctional family. Richey ran the organization with an iron fist, and members of the band, who had been so loyal to Mom that they left George Jones for her, were leaving or thinking of leaving. The happy banter on the bus was turning into chronic grousing. Richey nitpicked everyone. It was almost as though he was trying to run them off.

JAN SMITH WAS a few minutes late arriving at Mom's house for the beginning of a road trip to California, and Richey wanted to leave without her. Mom refused, and kept the bus parked until Jan got there. Jan felt that he punished her the whole trip, carping about one inconsequential thing after another. While they were in Los Angeles, Mom and Richey went out with friends every night and left her to baby-sit Georgette, who, because she was not yet in school, traveled with them a lot.

That had never happened before. It was Mom's custom

either to include Jan in her social plans or to leave her free to spend her time as she pleased. Never had she imposed on her to baby-sit.

"I knew he was going to fire me, so I quit at the end of that tour," Jan said. "Even if he didn't fire me, it was just getting too stressful to be around him. There was always some crisis or some ruckus."

Reflecting on that period years later, Jan said she had managed to stay with the troupe for a few years, but only because Mom had, in a sense, protected her from Richey. Mom's influence over him dwindled as his domination increased.

Nan Crafton replaced her sister as Mom's hair stylist, but her experiences with Richey were just as unpleasant. One night, as the bus was rolling into Provo, Utah, where Mom was going to do a television show with Donnie and Marie Osmond, Richey jumped on Nan for no good reason.

It was her job not only to fix Mom's hair, but also to style the twenty-five wigs she used when there wasn't time to redo her hair between numbers. She had always done a superb job and I never once heard Mom complain about her work.

That night, though, Richey was spoiling for a row.

"Nan, how many of those wigs are done?" he demanded.

The question just came from nowhere. It wasn't an issue that had ever been raised before. Not recalling exactly how many she had styled, Nan replied, "I can get her through the day."

Mom rarely used more than a couple of wigs during a show. Three or four would have been very unusual, let alone twenty-five.

"Don't you ever get in my presence without every one of those wigs done," Richey snapped.

Over time, Nan began to believe that getting rid of her was exactly what Richey had in mind. By getting rid of everyone who represented Mom's past life, her life before him, Richey was consolidating his hold over her.

And, yet, he could show extraordinary kindness to her old pals.

One year Richey learned that Jan's son, Cannon, wanted a set of drums for his birthday—a gift Jan could not afford. Richey bought the drums in Florida, flew them to Nashville on a Learjet, rented a limousine and delivered them to Jan's house.

It was that contradictory nature that drove those around him up the wall. One minute he was a tyrant, and the next he was Santa Claus. To people like Jan, even knowing that his generosity was fueled by Tammy Wynette's earnings did not dampen their appreciation of the gestures.

LISTENING TO JOHN's tales of trouble in the Wynette camp was unsettling—and he hadn't yet told me all of it.

He finally divulged the worst revelation after a particularly long road trip. "I'm worried about your mother," he said.

"What about her?" I asked, thinking he was referring to her abdominal pains. He was, but only indirectly.

"I'm worried about the amount of painkillers she's taking. She just seems to need them all the time."

When I lived at home, I was aware that she had taken various drugs for pain off and on, as her problems came and went, and as one surgery followed another. But I had thought of that as routine medical treatment, not a cause for concern.

"What do you mean, *all the time*?" I asked him.

"I think she's addicted to the stuff," he said.

I felt as though I had swallowed a brick. What made him think that? Just certain things, he said. The way Richey would take her aside and give her a shot even if John hadn't heard her ask for one and she didn't appear to be suffering. The way her moods shifted so abruptly. She could be upbeat and having fun, but after a moment alone with Richey, she would slouch into lethargy. She could be sluggish and weary before a show, but give her a moment alone with Richey and she'd be wired like a Scud missile.

"It just bothers me that she's taking so much so often," John said.

I knew just enough about addictions to be acquainted with the denial factor, so I figured it would serve no purpose to discuss the issue directly with Mom. Instead, I talked to Gwen, who was nursing the same concerns, I soon found out. We talked to Jan and Nan and anyone else in the entourage who might confide in us.

Gradually, we began to get a picture of what was going on in the privacy of the bus's stateroom or backstage at her shows or in the hotels where they stayed while on tour. She was not taking painkillers just when she was in pain. She received injections at regular intervals, day in and day out, and often it was Richey who administered them to her. He was firmly in control of her life and career, but he could still be her benefactor.

Gwen and I tried to figure out if there was anything we could do to force her into a hospital for treatment of her addiction. Everyone we asked—doctors, lawyers, a couple of friends who had faced similar situations—told us that we were powerless. She had to seek treatment herself. Failing that, only her husband could take steps to have her committed. Legally, her children were out of the loop.

IN CONFRONTING THAT problem, or trying to, I formed an opinion about the true nature of my mother's relationship with her husband. There was a strange codependence between them that, I now believe, was anchored in fear, mutual fear.

Mom feared that without Richey her career would flounder and, more important, she would not have access to the drugs her addiction demanded. Richey's fear, I think, was that his gravy train would derail.

His musical brilliance would provide a good living in Nashville, but it would not sustain the lifestyle that he was enjoying with Tammy Wynette. Good songwriters and studio musicians can certainly afford the Cadillacs and Lexuses and other show wheels that Music Row practically demands, and they don't have to live in tract housing or shop at Dollar General, but most of them can't divide their time between a 17,000-square-foot mansion and a lavish beach house or hire a Learjet on a whim or cruise the Vegas Strip with a briefcase filled with a hundred grand in cash. Neither do they reside in the spotlight or near the seat of the industry's real power. Talent and name are two different things. Richey had one. Tammy Wynette had both.

Not for a minute do I believe, though, that Richey pursued my mother and married her solely for her money. My hunch is that money was never really a factor in his attraction to her. But once he had achieved the higher lifestyle, he quickly adapted to it, became wholly seduced by it and feared losing it. Before he married Mom, his career in the music business had reached its logical plateau. He was still relatively young (in his early forties), but minus Tammy, he faced the prospect of becoming just another fringe figure, a hanger-on in a fickle world where hanging on got tougher every year.

New faces came and went and new sounds rose and fell, but a big name was always bankable. Yesterday's heroes might age and fade, but if they were willing and able, they could still find lucrative work. And Tammy Wynette was a name—like Loretta Lynn or Dolly Parton or Barbara Mandrell or Reba McEntire—that would be around for a long time, long after the crossover hits were gone and the industry awards were being scooped up by younger voices.

Tammy meant security, not only for her husband but for the various members of his family who were on her payroll. I don't mean to suggest that he was a freeloader. From what I have seen and from what I have been told by the members of Mom's crew, he worked as hard as she did, maybe harder. But she was the irreplaceable talent in the equation, not him.

What had always puzzled people close to her was that in their twenty-year marriage, Richey never made a serious attempt to nudge her into treatment. Assuming that he loved her and loved the lifestyle she afforded him, why did he accommodate her destructive behavior rather than insist that she defeat it?

My first glimpse at what may have been the answer to those questions came in the mid-1980s, in an incident that my sisters and I remember as the "briefcase fiasco."

It was an incident which may have demonstrated to Richey that his place in Tammy Wynette's life was not inexorable and that, given a clear head, she possessed the will and the courage to send him packing.

Fourteen

LESS THAN TWO years after Cathye Leshay left our house, Mom started trying to locate her. She wanted her back. Gwen and I were gone from home, but Tina was only thirteen and Georgette was seven, and they needed someone like Cathye around.

After Richey had essentially fired her, Cathye went back to teaching for one semester. Bored with that, she and a girlfriend, also a teacher, decided to take some time off and see something besides a classroom. They lived for a year in Hawaii, on the island of Maui, before Cathye returned to Gadsden, Alabama, where most of her family lived.

She found a job, leased an apartment and was barely settled in when Mom located her.

"Hey, babe, what are you doing?" Mom asked on the phone.

"Just got in from work," Cathye said, a little surprised to hear from her old employer.

"Did you have fun in Maui?" Mom said.

"I sure did—" Cathye said.

Before she could say anything more, Mom interrupted. "Please come back to work for me," she pleaded.

Their parting had been amicable. Cathye had been understanding of Richey's desire to dismantle the sorority that the house had become, but now she also understood Mom's need to have her back. So many members of Richey's family had taken up residence in her house that she was surrounded by wall-to-wall in-laws. She adored Richey's family, Cathye knew, but she longed for old familiar faces and she seemed to miss the conviviality of the old days. And she needed someone to look after Tina and Georgette.

"You've had your fun," Mom coaxed, "now I want you to come back, and if you do, I want you to stay with me till we die—or you find a cute guy."

Cathye hesitated. "I've just signed a lease on an apartment and . . . " she said.

"Just think about it, that's all I ask," Mom said, and then added the kicker. "By the way, we're going to Europe on a tour and I want you to go with us."

Cathye would later tell me that Mom certainly knew how to tantalize a little girl from Alabama who had never been anywhere except Maui. Her boss let her out of the job contract, and she solved the lease problem by moving her mother into the apartment.

By the time she came back, Mom and Richey had moved out of the big house on Franklin Road and were living in Hendersonville, in a house on Old Hickory Lake. After a year there, Mom decided she wanted to move to Florida permanently and live on the beach.

The only obstacle to the move was Georgette. She was about to enter high school, and at that age leaving friends and familiar places behind is difficult. Mom made a promise to her: if she would accept the move to Florida, she would not have to move again until she had graduated from high school. Georgette agreed.

For me, it was a terrific arrangement. John and I and Sophia, our first child, were waiting to buy a condo in Florida. Mom invited us to live with her until our new place was ready. Gwen, by then, was newly married, and she and her husband, Zack, were talking about moving from Colorado to Florida.

At long last, it seemed, there was peace and tranquillity in the family. Mom's dependence on painkillers still troubled us, but I was hopeful that, amid the slower pace of life in a small seaside town, with Cathye there to assist with her children, she might have time to reflect on what she was doing to herself and wean herself from the drugs.

The illusion that something had changed for the better didn't last long.

In the fall of 1984, Gwen was at home in Colorado when Mom called.

"I want you to come to Florida," she said.

"What's wrong?" Gwen asked, recognizing from the stress in her voice that this wasn't an invitation to a beach party.

"Richey is setting up all these accounts and taking out lines of credit," Mom said. "I don't know what's going on and I'm scared."

Gwen and Zack flew down to Florida and, once there,

realized there was a full-blown crisis under way. Though she tried to conceal it around Richey, Mom was distraught over her lack of control over her money.

"I want to divorce Richey," she told Gwen over lunch.

Oh, brother, Gwen thought, here we go again. But this smacked of more than just another of our mother's marital complications. Gwen and Zack decided to abandon Colorado right away and take up residence in the beach house. She even got a job at Sunrise Savings and Loan Association, where Richey had established lines of credit for some of his investments.

Gwen found out about one account that was in the name of "Richardson and Richardson." That sounded to her like something involving Richey and his brother, but when she confronted him about it, he told her that the names, in fact, were his and Mom's.

"Don't forget," he said, "my legal name is Richardson and so is your mother's."

Having no real evidence to contradict him, Gwen accepted his explanation.

Mom didn't, though, and she persisted in her belief that he was concealing things from her. One day she told Zack, "I want you to do something for me. I want you to find Richey's briefcase and break into it," she said.

Zack blinked hard and said, "I can't do that."

"Yes you can," Mom insisted. "Just make it look like a theft or a burglary."

Gwen joined the argument. "Mom, that's crazy," she said.

But Tammy Wynette had her mind made up. She would find a way. A day or two later, she invited John and me to go for a ride, and as we drove around, she told us she suspected that Richey was up to something and she wanted us to help her find out what it was. She said she would get him out of the house and we could break into the briefcase, which he always kept locked, remove the contents to see if her money was involved and throw the case into the ocean.

She was so insistent and so convinced that it contained something she ought to know about that we agreed to do it.

The next morning, Gwen went to work as usual and Cathye had taken Georgette to school. John also had something to do that day, so that left Zack, Tina and me in the house to do the deed. None of us liked the idea and we were scared to death, but we were prepared to go through with it for Mom's sake. Mom made up some excuse for Richey to take her somewhere, and we watched as they drove out of sight.

We discussed the potential consequences of what we were about to do, ultimately reassuring ourselves that it was in our mother's best interest. We were about to retrieve the briefcase from Richey's office when we heard their car drive up.

Apparently, Mom had also been weighing the consequences of her little plot and had become frightened. This was to form a pattern in years to come. She would muster the courage to defy Richey and then, fearful that she couldn't get along without him, she would crater.

That morning, she cratered hard. Just a couple of miles away from the house, she confessed to him, telling him everything. He wheeled the car around, hurried back to the house and ran through the door in a rage. Hell broke loose. He yelled and screamed at everyone.

When Tina, the most combative of the siblings, stepped up to confront him, he pushed her over a sofa and began menacing her. Zack tried to pull him off and the scuffle continued through the house, with Mom yelling, "Stop! Stop!" to no avail.

I was furious and frightened. Richey stormed around the house like a madman. I ducked into a bathroom and when he came in after me, I threw myself against him, pinning him to the wall. "I hate you! I hate you!" I screamed.

Zack again tried to restrain Richey, who was ranting that he wanted all of us out of his house, that he was going to have us all thrown in jail. I ran out of the room and into the kitchen, where I called Gwen at work.

"Don't come home," I told her. "Richey's gone crazy. He's going to have us arrested."

When things calmed down a little, Richey did, in fact, call the cops.

The downside was that Mom stood beside Richey and ordered all of us out of the house. We could not even pack. We would have to come back later, with a police chaperone, to get our things. John and I checked into a motel in West Palm Beach and stayed there for a week. Gwen and Zack went back to Colorado and Tina went to Nashville.

I didn't talk to my mother for several months after that, and neither did Gwen or Tina. We all felt that she had set us up and then betrayed us, letting us take the fall for her scheme. My judgment now is less severe. Richey had become a crutch she believed she couldn't live without. And, to him, I believe she was the mother lode he was loath to surrender.

Now I am convinced that Richey never sought help for her addiction because he suspected that if she was in full control of her faculties, she might do more than plot against his briefcase.

* * *

As THE WEEKS and months passed, I kept expecting my mother to call to apologize, but she never did. It was six or seven months before any of us heard from her. When we did, she was calling to tell us that Richey's father had died.

No mention was made of the briefcase incident, but she saw the mourning period as an opportunity to reestablish contact with her daughters and make amends for the unpleasant episode she had instigated. Our anger had dissipated by then and we, too, were ready to end the estrangement. But Gwen and I determined that if we were going to return to her fold, we would not be idle bystanders as she destroyed herself with narcotics. Whether she liked it or not, whether Richey liked it or not, we would agitate for treatment.

It would not be easy. Her denial was absolute and she was willfully oblivious to all evidence of addiction. She had taken so many injections that it had become nearly impossible to find a vein to receive the needle, so she resorted to shooting up between her toes. Apparently, even that did not give her pause. In the early 1980s, a writer named Dolly Carlisle was working on a book about George Jones, and in an interview with my mother, the question of her drug use came up.

"I've depended on Demerol, plus a lot of other medications, to get me through an awful lot of shows and a lot of pain," Mom said. "There's been many nights when I thought I would die if I had to go on stage and I depended on pain pills to get me through."

At the same time she admitted "depending" on narcotics, she denied being "addicted" to them. It was a bizarre semantic waltz that enabled her to sidestep reality.

Occasionally, I mentioned to Richey that something had to be done and he seemed wholly sympathetic. Once, in fact, he called and confided that "your mother needed help," and at other times he talked to Gwen and me about taking her to the Betty Ford Center. I was not unsympathetic to his dilemma—pressing the issue would only provoke her wrath—but I held to the hope that, as her husband, he would find a way to do what had to be done.

There was a lot going on in Mom's life during that period. She wasn't scoring the number-one hits anymore, but her touring schedule was still busy. Her autobiography was made into a successful television movie; she recorded "Sometimes When We Touch," a duet with Mark Gray that became a Top 10 hit, and she joined the cast of the CBS soap opera *Capitol*, playing Darlene Stankowski, a waitress and the romantic interest of a character played by Rory Calhoun. It was also during that time that she and Richey were deciding that living on the beach in Florida was not very practical. It was a little too far from the recording studios and concert venues of Nashville. And, with the acting gig, Southern California was becoming more and more her center of gravity.

Gwen and I kept prodding Richey, but the months passed and we became preoccupied with our own lives. In the fall of 1986, when she got sick in California, I was unable to go to her side.

She was hospitalized at the Eisenhower Medical Center in Palm Springs for yet more to do with her recurring stomach problems. Gwen, Tina and Georgette flew to California to be with her, and it turned out to be a fortuitous family gathering.

Because the Betty Ford Center is located on the grounds of the Eisenhower Center, rumors began circulating immediately that she was being treated for drug addiction. Her publicist issued the standard denials, but at least the rumors had raised an issue that the family could expound upon.

With help from the doctors who were treating her stomach problem, Mom was persuaded to check into the Betty Ford Center for a treatment regimen that would take six weeks. She canceled all of her shows for the remainder of the year and began the program a few days later.

All of us were ecstatic. This was what we had prayed for, for her to confront her addiction and whip it. But it was still hard for her to acknowledge the truth. Her publicist, Kent Arwood, issued a statement about her admission to the center. "It is not an addiction, but it's a problem they wanted to nip in the bud before it got out of hand," he said. With so many famous people owning up to longtime addictions, why was it so hard for her to do so? It wasn't as if she was a junkie. Most of the country-music crowd knew about her chronic ailments and her reliance on painkillers and were sympathetic. Most of her fans probably also knew, and they certainly didn't judge her to be a drug addict.

Three weeks into the program, Mom left the Ford Center.

Apparently, she had developed total intestinal blockage. Previous surgeries had severely narrowed the opening where food leaves the stomach and enters the intestines. With food unable to leave her stomach, her abdomen began to swell painfully. She underwent emergency surgery and was hooked up to breathing and feeding tubes for the next five weeks, during which time she also received large doses of painkillers. Any progress she may have made in the Ford Center was lost.

At first, I was a little suspicious. She had not gone happily to the treatment program and I knew, as she did, that withdrawal could be a nightmare. Could she have faked the stomach trouble just to get painkillers?

The answer turned out to be *no*. In short order, my mother underwent an eight-hour operation at the Mayo Clinic to correct the damage from previous surgeries. Doctors removed a quarter of her stomach and parts of her intestines and tried to reconstruct a normal digestive tract.

The surgeons were only partially successful. That meant Tammy would see the rooms of many more hospitals in the years to come.

If scalpels were destined to remain an integral part of her existence, then so were painkillers.

Fifteen

NOTWITHSTANDING THE BRIEFCASE incident and Mom's concerns about Richey's control of her money, the years in Jupiter had their upside—for Mom and for Georgette. Cathye Leshay had checked out the schools and selected one for Georgette—a private Christian school which Georgette adapted to perfectly. In fact, Cathye swore my sister was the most popular girl in the school. She was a cheerleader and homecoming attendant every year and was the odds-on favorite to be homecoming queen her senior year. Mom and Richey were away a lot, but every year, Mom flew home to drive Georgette in the homecoming parade in her convertible.

When she was home in Florida, Mom could completely relax. The citizens of Jupiter were accustomed to celebrities living among them—Burt Reynolds's ranch was nearby and Perry Como had a house not far from Mom's. She could go wherever she pleased and not have to worry about being bothered by anyone.

John and I lived about forty miles south in Del Rey
Beach and, with the briefcase thing behind us, Mom came
to visit us a lot. Sophia was her only granddaughter at the
time, and Mom was the quintessential grandmother. She
showered my daughter with clothes and other gifts, photographed her profusely and fussed over her constantly.

Her health was still a seesaw. One day she would be
feeling great, and the next, Richey would be rushing her
off to the hospital. Work was becoming more difficult.
Cathye has told me of seeing her go on stage to deliver a
powerful performance only to collapse in the wings afterward, necessitating another rush to the emergency room.

Sometimes her breath would be so shallow and her pain
so great that she would sit off stage connected to an IV and
respiratory tubes. When it was time to go on, she'd be disconnected. Immediately after performing, she would return to the tubes.

Those periods would pass, followed by a period of energy and creativity.

On one of those good days, she and Cathye were driving home from a grocery shopping trip, and as they talked,
Cathye uttered a line—"I'm afraid I'd live through it"—in
reference to something, and then she laughed and said,
"That sounds like a song title."

The next day, Mom was standing by the piano when
Cathye heard her say, "Come here."

As Cathye approached, Mom sat down at the piano and
said, "Listen to our song."

She had composed the melody and written the lyrics
that morning. She later recorded it and it was released on
the B side of *Unwed Fathers*.

She gave Cathye half the royalties and, whenever

Cathye was present at one of her shows, half the credit, introducing her to the audience as the coauthor.

Cathye enjoyed those years, and I know she was a little sad when they ended. But, sometime before Mom's aborted stay at the Betty Ford Center, she and Richey, who had never seemed to share Mom's enthusiasm for Florida, decided to sell the beach house and move back to Nashville.

To keep her word to Georgette, Mom rented a condo in Jupiter so Georgette could stay there with Cathye until she graduated in 1988.

But something happened to Georgette on the way to her senior year. She fell in love with a guy a year ahead of her in school. After graduation, he was going to enroll at Oral Roberts University in Tulsa, Oklahoma, and study to be a minister.

Determined to go with him, Georgette decided to graduate a year early, earning her senior-year credits by correspondence while she was still a junior.

Cathye was adamantly opposed to the idea.

"Don't do this," she pleaded with Mom and Richey. "Don't let her lose a year of her youth."

Richey pretty much stayed out of the decision, and Cathye was aware that Georgette had a way of getting her way with Mom.

"She's going to be homecoming queen," Cathye argued. "You're going to deprive her of some of the happiest memories she will ever have."

As she suspected, her invocations were futile. Cathye was aware that she was pleading her case to a woman who had had a restless adolescence, had married young and had struck out on her own while her friends were still cramming for finals.

Georgette prevailed and actually pulled it off, earning her junior- and senior-year credits in a single year. But by then her romance with the ORU student had cooled. She went to the University of Northern Alabama, occasionally going on the road as a singer opening shows for George Jones.

When she left, Cathye's work was done. As she was vacating the condo, she found a letter my mother had left for her.

"Thank you for helping me raise my girls," Mom wrote. "The reason God didn't give you children is because He knew I needed you."

The next year, Cathye married a contractor she had met in Jupiter, a young man Richey had hired to do some work on the beach house, and they later settled in Miami.

She didn't see Mom for several years, then one day in 1995 she got a phone call.

"Richey and I are going to be in Fort Lauderdale for a show," Mom said. "Why don't you and David come up?"

Cathye was looking forward to the reunion. She had grown fond not only of Mom, but also of Richey. She has told me that she never saw them fight, never saw Richey do anything unkind toward Mom. He let it be known to any and all that he was the boss, and Cathye saw that as his way of protecting my mother.

Cathye and her husband drove up to the hall where Mom's show was scheduled and found the bus parked outside. When they walked in, Cathye nearly lost her composure. David squeezed her hand to steady her.

The Tammy Wynette she was looking at was a frail old woman, a ghost of the woman she had lived with for ten years.

* * *

TAMMY WYNETTE'S RETURN to Nashville was another roller coaster.

On the upswing, she released a successful new album, *Higher Ground,* with the help of a flock of young stars. Vince Gill, Ricky Van Shelton, Rodney Crowell, Ricky Skaggs, Emmylou Harris, and The O'Kanes trooped into the studio to sing backup for her. A few old hands, like Gene Watson and Vern Gosdin, dropped in, too, and the result had the critics oozing praise. While they were hailing her return to the top of the charts after a two-year absence, she was making plans to go to England to record an album with the London Symphony. Her music was starting to change, and so was her appearance. A new, shorter hairdo gave her a hipper, more sophisticated look and she began to shed her hallmark sequin gowns for more casual stage clothes.

As always seemed to be the case for Tammy, bad news came on the heels of triumph. This time, trouble in Jupiter soon stalked her back to Nashville.

THE HOUSEKEEPER OPENED the door that Tuesday morning in late September 1988 and found herself facing a group of serious-looking men in suits and ties. One of them displayed a badge and ID card and said, "I'm Chuck Goggin with the U.S. Marshals Service."

She looked at the badge and back into the eyes of the federal cop. "Yes?" she said.

"Is this the residence of George and Virginia Richardson?" he asked.

"Yes."

"May I speak with one of them?"

"They're not here," she said, explaining that Mom and Richey were in California.

"I have a court order directing me to take custody of this property and all personal possessions in the house," he said. He showed her the court order, and the other men entered the house and began videotaping everything inside.

That was the beginning of a scramble to settle, once and for all, the consequences of financial dealings that had begun years earlier in Jupiter. I don't know if Mom knew about the transactions or if they were among those she had suspected Richey of concealing from her, but, either way, the Federal Savings and Loan Insurance Corp., which regulated thrifts, claimed that Mom and Richey owed $900,000 to the Sunrise Savings and Loan Association, which was now defunct.

It had been shut down by regulators because of fraudulent activities. That was around the time that the whole S&L industry was about to collapse from bad real estate and energy loans, bad management and outright corruption. After Sunrise was closed, three of its executives were indicted for conspiracy and fraud. As regulators pored over the thrift's books, they found two loans, totaling $750,000, to George and Virginia Richardson.

The money had been used to invest in two shopping centers in Boynton Beach. After months of dickering back and forth, the FSLIC went to court in early 1988 and sued for the money. For some reason Mom and Richey had not appeared when the case came up for trial. Therefore, the FSLIC won a default judgment.

One of Richey's Nashville lawyers then began negotiating with the regulators. Richey claimed that the loans had been paid but "some shady dealings" by Sunrise executives had kept the payments from showing up on the books. The lawyer thought the talks were continuing; apparently, he had no inkling of the FSLIC's impatience with the whole thing—no idea, that is, until that Tuesday morning. He also received a call from the Marshals Service.

"We have a court order to seize Tammy Wynette's property," the marshal told him. "There will be a van at the house at twelve-thirty, if you want to watch the possessions being removed."

Goggin stationed marshals on the property to guard it until a complete inventory could be conducted the next day. "Until I'm told differently, that's my property," he told a reporter.

Fines and penalties and other costs had pushed the total of the FSLIC claim up to $900,000 by the time the writ was issued in September, and the lawyer advised Mom and Richey of their options by telephone.

That afternoon, another lawyer acting on their behalf filed an emergency bankruptcy petition in federal court, effectively freezing whatever action the FSLIC and the U.S. Marshals were planning next. The guards were withdrawn from the property and the negotiations with the regulators resumed.

The entire thing was distressing to my mother. By filing for bankruptcy, she had to enter into the public record a list of all her assets and liabilities and a breakdown of her monthly living expenses. The press didn't overlook the smallest detail of it. Not only was the world given the suspicion that she had somehow cheated Sunrise Savings, it was given a peek into the one part of her life she had previously managed to keep private.

Among other things, she had to reveal a $50,000 loan from Burt Reynolds. When I saw that in the newspapers, it surprised me because she had confided in me once that

Richey had asked her to borrow money from Burt and that she was resisting.

"I just can't do it," she'd said.

From the press reports, I concluded it was likely that Richey had gotten his way. Now it was a public record and all she could do was suffer through the embarrassment.

Richey issued one public statement through Mom's publicist, but it shed no light on the truth about the Sunrise loans.

"Tammy and I are merely the victims of people who are sharper with the pencil than she and I are," he said.

Over the next few weeks, her lawyers managed to reach a settlement with the FSLIC. Mom and Richey agreed to pay $450,000 and the case was closed.

Nearly a year later, two former officers of the S&L were convicted of fraud and conspiracy and sent to federal prison. Two of the shopping-center developers pleaded guilty to similar charges and also got jail time.

The headline in the *Nashville Banner* said: WYNETTE VINDICATED.

Many times, I wondered if that entire episode could have been avoided if she had not aborted her plan to break into Richey's briefcase back in 1984.

MOM WAS FOND of getting dressed up and going to the Sunset Grill or some other trendy restaurant with her friends, so Martha Dettwiller was puzzled one day when Mom suggested that they eat at a local place that was sort of a poor man's McDonald's. As late as the early nineties, they still had twenty-nine-cent hamburgers, or something like that.

Afterward, they were driving around and Mom told Martha, "We had to take the band off salary."

That also puzzled Martha. "Why are you telling me this?" she asked.

"I want you to know that we don't have any money," Mom said.

"Sweetheart . . . the band has to have an income," Martha said, almost sputtering.

"We just can't pay them," she sighed.

It was inconceivable that Tammy Wynette was broke. There was no doubt that settling with the FSLIC had caused a financial pinch, but she still had the Franklin Road mansion, which was worth $1.5 million. She had property in Red Bay, Alabama, and in Malden, Missouri, worth a combined $126,000. "Stand by Your Man" had become the biggest-selling record in country-music history—it was still being recorded by other artists—and was, I assume, earning generous royalties. And she was still working, probably more than her fragile health could tolerate.

Mom was convinced they were living paycheck to paycheck, and she went along with the austerity measures Richey imposed.

If her checking account ran low, she had to call Sylvia, Richey's assistant, and ask that a deposit be made. Sylvia paid her bills.

Once, Mom and Martha went to a dress shop and one of the managers steered Martha aside and whispered, "Tammy's bill hasn't been paid." They were too embarrassed to tell Mom, so they passed that chore to Martha.

Another time, they were shopping for clothes for Georgette, who had just given birth to twins, and Mom's credit card was rejected. She fished through her purse until she found one that worked, and when they got to the house, Mom insisted on leaving the clothes in the car so Richey would not know she had bought them. Eventually, she temporarily stopped buying clothes for her daughters and grandchildren—a favorite activity—and, instead, made garments from fabric she bought at Hancock's.

She had always been generous with her children, giving us cash for vacations or other luxuries, but that, too, changed. She still gave us small amounts of money now and then, but was very secretive about it. If we were at the house, she would wait until Richey was out of the room and then slip money to us, or tell us where she had hidden money for us.

She had surrendered so much control over her affairs to her husband that she didn't seem to know what her financial status was. When she saw contradictions, she was more confused than angered by them. In those dire straits, she wondered how Richey could afford to send money to Elton John for an AIDS benefit. How could Richey afford to charter a Learjet to join her at a show, to which she had traveled on the bus?

Most important, why did they need such a large house for such a small family?

When they decided to sell the big house on Franklin Road, there were no children left at home and her friends didn't come around as much as they once had.

"I would be happy with a nice town house," she told Gwen.

Richey said they needed a large house, a place where they could entertain. They ended up moving just a few miles down Franklin Road, to a house that was smaller, but expansive nonetheless. Sitting at the base of a sloping driveway on a large, wooded lot, their new dwelling had been owned by Hank Williams Sr. It was, without question, fit for a star of his caliber.

Sixteen

ARTISTS SUCH AS Tammy Wynette were finding out in the early 1990s, if not before, that their turf in country music was shrinking. The executive offices of the recording companies were being purged of traditional country-music lions and younger barons were being installed in their place.

People who were nothing short of legendary—Charley Pride, Waylon Jennings, George Jones, Loretta Lynn, Dolly Parton and many others—were dumped by their labels. In the seventies and eighties, they had made country the hottest music in America, and even after they qualified for AARP membership, most were in as fine a voice as they had ever been. Yet they couldn't buy a recording contract.

The new Nashville brain trust was made up mostly of fugitives from rock and pop, and they wanted to blur the lines between those species and country. *Expand the market* was the marching order; by blurring the lines, you could bring in new fans if those fans didn't care for real country music.

The sound was less important than the sell. It was the age of the video, and what sold, they believed, was youth, tight jeans, smooth skin, big hats and sex appeal. It was nice if a slinky babe could sing, but if she couldn't, a good sound mixer could cover for her.

Some of the new executives knew next to nothing about country music and apparently had no inclination to learn. One of my favorite stories is one I heard about a producer and a new studio genius discussing the possibility of John Berry recording the old Patsy Cline standard "I Fall to Pieces." There could be a problem getting rights to the song, the producer said.

"Well," said the boy wonder, "why don't we just have Patsy come in and record it."

Patsy died in 1963.

Mom's music had always been pretty hard-core traditionalist, tear-in-my-beer, dance-hall melancholy mainstays. As much as anyone, maybe more than most, she was a candidate for being imprisoned by her musical past.

I'VE NEVER ASKED Charlton Heston, but it would not surprise me if he sometimes comes across people who think it was really he who talked to the burning bush and carried the tablets down from the mountain and parted the Red Sea, due to his portrayal of Moses in *The Ten Commandments*.

People have a tendency to associate actors with the roles they play, singers with the songs they sing, artists with the paintings they create. Sometimes, it seems, the association is so powerful that the line between artist and art is completely lost. Fess Parker died at the Alamo, you know. Or was that John Wayne?

So it was with "Stand by Your Man." It was the biggest song of Tammy Wynette's career, the kind of signature work that many performers spend a lifetime striving for. It came to her early in her career and it cemented her place in country-music lore by becoming the biggest-selling single by a woman in the history of that genre. It gave her a following outside the confines of country music, and it made her fabulously wealthy.

Yet . . . sometimes, it drove her to distraction—not the song, but the perception of it, the rigorous debate over it, its being the object of such interminable analysis and profound misunderstanding. To many, Mom's life was expected to mirror the lyrics, even though those with such expectations had little understanding of the message those lyrics conveyed.

Many times, Mom wanted to grab some critic by the collar, shake him or her and say, "It's just a song!" But not even my mother could have anticipated the hubbub that would result from a stray comment—uttered by a presidential contender's wife under the glare of national TV— nearly a quarter century after "Stand by Your Man" 's release.

THE ENDEARING QUALITY of country music is that it comes from the heart—either that or those who create it manage to fake that candor superbly. And what comes from the heart is ephemeral, of the moment. Hank Williams wrote many of his songs in a matter of minutes, tapping out a beat on the dashboard of his car while the words gushed forth like blood from a severed vein. Merle Haggard has written in the same way. A particular mood—melancholy or anger or joy or pride or any other of a dozen sensations—speaks to the creative force. Experience, the sum total of the artist's existence, is a kind of filter through which the logic of the art is passed. The art is truth as best mood and experience can express it.

Here's what I know about that marvelous song: Billy Sherrill had heard the line "stand by your man" on a television show and, to him, it possessed a certain resonance. A lot of good songs begin that way, with just a line, a phrase, a throwaway thought. "Okie from Muskogee," the song that made Haggard a superstar, is one of them. It happened one night when Haggard was passing through Oklahoma and stopped in Checotah to visit an uncle he had not seen in a long time. When his group got back on the road, their bus passed a sign pointing the way to Muskogee.

Merle and the band members were well into smoke by then and someone made the crack, "I'll bet they don't smoke marijuana in Muskogee." Within fifty miles, the song was completed.

"Stand by Your Man" was a little like that.

Billy Sherrill had written down the line and carried it with him while he tried to blow it into a full composition. He had a chorus . . .

Stand by your man
Give him two arms to cling to
And something warm to come to
When nights are cold and lonely.

Stand by your man
And show the world you love him.

Keep givin' all the love you can.
Stand by your man.

Some critics have interpreted those lines as dripping
with sexism, although Mom never accepted that analysis
and, frankly, neither do I. It just sounds like an expression
of reasonable marital values to me. If the genders were
flipped, would feminists find it objectionable? Stand by
your woman. Stand by your man. Be true to your school.
Support your local police. As far as I am concerned, those
lines are extraordinarily innocuous.

But Sherrill still needed the meat of the song, the verse
to set up the chorus—and that's where a lot of the misunderstanding came in. At a recording session one day, he
and Mom went to a private room upstairs and sat down at a
piano. What would a woman say about this idea of standing by the man she loved? Maybe her own experience, as
much as her ideology, took over. Together, they composed:

Sometimes it's hard to be a woman,
Givin' all your love to just one man.
You'll have bad times,
And he'll have good times
Doin' things that you don't understand.

But if you love him you'll forgive him
Even though he's hard to understand.
And if you love him
Oh, be proud of him
'Cause, after all, he's just a man.

Tammy Wynette had been through a lot with the men
she loved, or thought she loved, and she had put up with

her share of rascals, forgiving more than one of them almost to the point of foolishness. But I think her honest belief was that men are imperfect creatures who need the strength of a woman to make them whole. *After all, he's just a man.*

She was not the kind of person driven to make political statements or to intellectualize the cosmic significance of her feelings. Loyalty, she believed, was essential to a relationship. So were forgiveness and tolerance. Anyone who knew Tammy Wynette, though, knew that those qualities were not limitless. She had stood by her men until she could stand no more and then she regrouped, relying on her own independence and self-reliance. She raised her children. She ran her business. She made tough decisions and didn't just survive, she prospered—in a game where the deck was stacked against *girl singers.*

For that reason, she was appalled by the criticism of the so-called feminists of that era. In the late 1960s, the Women's Liberation Movement was a fierce sisterhood with the armies of the ages deployed against it. It was radical and strident, as was probably necessary, and seized any opportunity to advance the feminist creed.

What an opportunity this was. Some poor, naive little hillbilly wench preaching the gospel of female subservience wasn't just an opportunity, it was a keg begging to be tapped.

What was, in my opinion, a moment of unfeigned virtue—*give him a break, he's just a man*—became anathema to the cause of gender equality. *Newsweek* called her music "songs of non-liberation." *The Village Voice* called her "pre-feminist," and *Country Music* magazine would write of her "old lapdog allegiance to the stronger sex."

Even after the song won a Grammy Award and became

a classic (it was recorded by such diverse artists as Loretta Lynn, Henry Mancini, Lynn Anderson, Lyle Lovett, The Chipmunks and Lawrence Welk), the controversy droned on. Every time Tammy Wynette broke up with a boyfriend or divorced a husband, some columnist or commentator would contrast the art and the artist. "Tammy Wynette doesn't stand by her man." How many times have I heard or read that tired old line?

By the spring of 1992 "Stand by Your Man" was the subject of a long, scholarly analysis in the quarterly *Popular Music and Society.* I was amazed that such intellectual depths could be plumbed on "just a song."

"Yes, the song is an ironic statement expressing a woman's ambivalence over her position vis-à-vis men. But there are other aspects of the song that suggest transcendent meaning that knits the ironic conflict into a broader fabric," wrote Kenneth E. Morris, a sociology professor at the University of Georgia. "In particular, there is a sense that ultimately the irony is subsumed by the lament of the song's first line: 'Sometimes it's hard to be a woman.' The ambivalence expressed by the song is, after all, a deep and troubling one, and the song exudes a sense of sadness. And for all the force of the chorus, it remains appended illogically to the verse. It seems not so much to answer the verse as to deepen and enlarge it. In all, there is a pathos and tragedy about the song that is not dispelled by the chorus. Confronting this sense of the song as one that deploys irony only en route to expressing a deeper existential pathos, one is tempted to search for a way to unite the conflict of the song into a deeper unifying gestalt."

Whew! I could never picture my mother reading that piece and nodding thoughtfully at the notion of existential pathos and unifying gestalt. It was pleasing to her, though, that Professor Morris's sociological ruminations wound their way to her own view of the song.

It may have been a "gender polemic," he wrote, but "more deeply, it is a lament over the human condition from a woman's perspective." The fans who devoured the song "may have liked it not for the ideology it articulated, but for the experience it expressed."

I suspect that the publication of his article was inspired by the way "Stand by Your Man" leapt back into the headlines, but unfortunately, Professor Morris would not have the last word.

MOM AND RICHEY were lying in bed that Sunday evening in 1992 watching a seminal moment in American television. An Arkansas politician named Bill Clinton, accompanied by his wife, Hillary, was appearing on the TV newsmagazine *60 Minutes* to talk about their personal lives. His campaign for president had been shaken by disclosures of his affair with Gennifer Flowers, and rather than dodge the cameras and prying questions of the press, he and his wife elected to confront them, to come clean with the electorate and hope for forgiveness.

As much attention would be focused on Hillary as on the would-be president. She was the wronged woman who had forgiven the rascal. Was it sincere absolution or political expediency? If the American people sensed phoniness on her part or his, the game might be over and they could go back to Arkansas and practice law.

Both were remarkably candid, and while Bill Clinton did not attempt to defend his misdemeanors, he was not overly contrite. There had been problems in their marriage, he said, but it was a personal matter to be resolved by him and his wife. Hillary's performance was just as convincing. She stayed with her husband because she loved him and she felt the marriage was worth saving. To remove any doubt that she was naive, subservient or imprisoned in the marriage, she said:

"I'm not sitting here, some little woman standing by my man like Tammy Wynette."

Hearing that, Mom sat up in bed and said, "What? Why is she involving me in this thing?"

She was truly offended by being held up once again, on national television, as a paragon of female weakness, dependency and insecurity. She had her publicist, Evelyn Shriver, prepare a statement demanding an apology on behalf of all women.

By the next day, Hillary was eager to do just that—apologize. She called the house, but Mom wouldn't talk to her, so she made a public statement: "I didn't mean to hurt Tammy Wynette as a person. I happen to be a country-western fan. If she feels like I've hurt her feelings, I'm sorry about that."

She continued to call the house, but Mom stubbornly refused to talk to her. After a few days, Burt Reynolds called. He was a friend of the Clintons and they had drafted him to help patch things up.

"Tammy," he pleaded, "you really should talk to Hillary Clinton."

That was all it took.

EIGHT MONTHS LATER, in September 1992, Richey got a call from someone representing Barbra Streisand, who was one of Mom's singing idols. Barbra was hosting a Democratic fund-raiser at her Bel Air home and the only record-ing artist she wanted on the show was Tammy Wynette.

I don't know if Mom was a Democrat or a Republican, and it didn't really matter. She had such adoration for Bar-bra Streisand that she would not have turned down the in-vitation, no matter who the party was for. Of course, she knew this bash would benefit the Clintons.

She flew to Los Angeles and met with Barbra.

"I can't believe you invited me to come out here and sing," Mom said.

"You're my favorite singer in the whole world," Barbra said.

"Well," Mom answered, "you're *my* favorite singer in the whole world."

It was decided that she would sing "America the Beauti-ful." The celebrities who had shelled out big bucks to at-tend the affair did not know who would perform. The invitations that Barbra sent out had said only that the pro-gram would feature a "special guest singer."

When the curtain opened, Hillary Clinton was sitting in the front row, next to Jack Nicholson. She looked up at Tammy Wynette and her jaw dropped.

The First Lady of Country Music and the future First Lady of the United States both knew the hatchet was truly buried.

THERE'S A FOOTNOTE to this story. Tammy Wynette and Hillary Clinton, it seemed, were both damned to be haunted by "Stand by Your Man."

In the summer of 1999, more than a year after Mom died, Hillary was testing the U.S. Senate waters in New

York and an editorial page column in the *New York Times*
noted the line she was trying to walk between her role as
First Lady and Senate wannabe. It talked about her whole
history being one of confusion "over where her identity as
good-listener wife ends and her own can-do political per-
sona begins."

Wrote the columnist Gail Collins:

"A lot of women who originally liked the idea of the
First Lady as a policy-driven political partner were cha-
grined when Mrs. Clinton turned out to be most popular
and successful when she played the role of supportive
wife. No doubt, Hillary Clinton felt pretty much the same
and she may be frightened of letting go of that restrictive
but comfortable identity."

The headline over the text: WHAT IS THIS, THE TAMMY
WYNETTE STRATEGY?

IF NASHVILLE WANTED to distance itself from Tammy
Wynette, she was determined to show it real distance. Late
in 1991, two wacky British pop singers/rappers known as
KLF saw an advertisement for Mom's London visit and
they sent her a message: TAMMY, STAND BY THE JAM (JAM
being the duo's former name).

They wanted to record a duet with her.

Anyone who had followed Mom's career closely would
not have been surprised by that. Her appeal had always
reached well outside the walls of country music. She had
even developed a sort of campy cult following in the most
unlikely subcultures. She had a large homosexual fan base,
for example, and she was probably the first country star to
hold benefits and give money for AIDS research. She got a
big kick out of a trip to New York when, after her show, a

group of gay men joined her at a restaurant and partied in Tammy Wynette drag.

At another show in New York, Wendy O. Williams, the lead singer for a punk-rock group called The Plasmatics, showed up. If you're not familiar with punk, I will tell you that Wendy was semi-maniacal; some newspaper critic once said that The Plasmatics made the Sex Pistols look like The Captain & Tennille. They had songs with titles like "Butcher Baby" and once blew up a Chevy Nova on the Tom Snyder late-night television show. You get the picture.

Sometimes Wendy's hair was cut into a platinum Mohawk, but that night in New York it was in purple spikes. What would possibly draw her to a Tammy Wynette show? After Mom finished her set, she noticed this strange-looking woman sitting by the stage, crying.

"What's the matter?" Mom asked her.

"Your voice makes me cry," Wendy said. "I can't stand it."

A sad footnote: The day after Mom died, Wendy put a bag over her head and killed herself with a .38-caliber pistol. It had nothing to do with Mom's death. Wendy left a suicide note that said, "For me, much of the world makes no sense, but my feelings about what I am doing ring loud and clear to an inner ear and a place where there is no self, only calm."

So, Mom had a knack for drawing a diverse and sometimes eccentric crowd into her orbit. She may have been flattered or merely amused and curious at the KLF invitation, or she may have wanted to show Nashville a Tammy Wynette it has rarely, if ever, seen.

The resulting single, "Justified & Ancient," was like nothing Mom had ever done before.

"I did it because it was something different," she told me. "I did it for fun. Those guys are crazy."

Crazy, I guess.

They cut the song in Nashville and then flew to London to tape the video. For that shoot, KLF (Bill Drummond and Jimmy Cauty) wore robes and hoods with rhinoceros masks. Mom wore a crown, a skin-tight turquoise mermaid dress and a Madonna-esque bustier. She perched on a mountain of stone—something like a Mayan pyramid—with writhing Zulu dancers at her feet and surreal graphics exploding around her. She later confided that she didn't know the meaning of any of it, but that didn't bother her. She later appeared on television with KLF, the boys dressed as twelve-foot ice-cream cones. Go figure.

She also didn't quite get the lyrics to the song about a strange place called "Mu Mu Land."

After the video was shot, Mom went to a restaurant with Mike Martinovich, who worked for her recording company.

"You know, I've been touring Europe since 1968," she told him. "I consider myself pretty cosmopolitan and a sophisticated traveler. I've been pretty much around the world . . . but where is this Mu Mu Land?"

Mike smiled. "Honey," he said, "it's in our minds . . . it's a state of mind."

THE FIRST LADY of Country had stepped out of country and conquered the world. "Justified & Ancient" shattered records around the globe. It topped the charts in eighteen nations, and in the United States it climbed to thirteen on the *Billboard* Hot 100 and went to single digits on the *Radio and Record*'s chart of pop music. Her previous pop-chart high had been No. 19. That was in 1968, with "Stand by Your Man."

Seventeen

"JUSTIFIED & ANCIENT" not only put Tammy Wynette back on the charts and boosted the demand for personal appearances, it seemed to energize her at a time when her vitality was being drained by another series of bile duct infections brought on by the same old condition: scarring left by previous surgeries.

Throughout the late winter and early spring of 1992, she fought off the attacks with painkillers and antibiotics and struggled through most of her schedule—but not all of it. In March, she was hospitalized in Perth and was forced to cancel the remainder of her Australian tour. As soon as she could walk around, though, she went back to work.

On May 4, she was on a Canadian tour when the infection raged out of control. She canceled a show in Brantford, Ontario, and checked into a hospital there overnight, and the next morning she and Richey set out on the tour bus for St. Louis and Barnes Hospital, which is affiliated with the Washington University Medical Center. The previous year, she had been treated at Barnes Hospital (the Center) for a similar problem by a young physician named James Wallis Marsh. They formed a quick bond, and from that point on, Marsh was her doctor.

Mom had a doctor in Nashville, but they had begun to part ways. He was concerned about the extent of her drug use and was increasingly reluctant to prescribe what she demanded. Finally, as things between them went from bad to worse, he encouraged her to find another physician. Meeting up with Marsh, at the time, seemed to be a godsend.

After she showed up in St. Louis that May afternoon, she was in the hospital for nearly a week and, when the infection did not respond to antibiotics, the doctors told her they would have to perform an intestinal bypass of the inflamed bile duct. The surgery took fourteen hours. For the next two days, her condition was listed as serious and she was not released for several more days.

Again, she went immediately back to work.

AMONG THOSE CLOSE to her, the opinion was almost unanimous: Tammy Wynette needed a long lull in her work schedule.

Gwen had recognized it long before. In the early 1990s, she had moved to Nashville to work for Mom and didn't like most of what she observed. She kept pressing for Richey to join us in another intervention and, finally, he halfheartedly agreed.

He and Mom were leaving on a tour. He told Gwen they would be back at four o'clock the following Monday. Gwen could schedule the intervention for then.

I got to the house early in the afternoon to go over some things with Gwen. Mostly we wanted to talk about the best way to convince Mom that what we were suggesting was the right thing.

She and Richey got home early, about two o'clock. When Richey found us at the house and we told him the meeting was set for two o'clock, he nearly choked. I don't think he believed we would go through with it.

Mom didn't take the news any better, but I think she and Richey realized they were stuck with us for the afternoon; they would at least go through the motions of hearing us out.

The meeting started at four. Richey was there, as were two counselors who would assist with the addiction treatment, and of course Gwen and I. We did our best to persuade Mom to seek treatment. Throughout the discussion, she was obviously put out with all of us.

We tried to reason with her, but she was defensive and defiant. We kept pressing and finally she snapped. "Fine . . . if that's the way you feel about it . . ." and stomped out of the room. Richey followed her and came back a couple of minutes later.

Looking at Gwen and me, he said, "Your mom said we were all crazy."

That was it. No treatment. Back to work. Gwen and I began to form the opinion that Richey did not push harder for treatment because he did not want to risk permanently alienating his wife and also because he was concerned about her earning no money for the time the treatment would take.

He went to some length to keep her health problems out of the public eye. One probable reason was that promoters are reluctant to book artists who may not be able to appear.

When shows had to be canceled due to Mom's ill health, he would instruct Gwen to give them a different reason.

Mom was pushing herself to exhaustion with Richey's cooperation and there was nothing we could do about it. Except dread where it was leading.

One morning, Richey called Gwen and said, "Your mom's missing." When he woke up, she was not in bed. He looked through the house and found no trace of her. "Don't call the police," he cautioned. "We can't let this get in the press."

While Richey called his relatives and some business associates to see if they had seen Mom, Gwen got in her car and cruised the neighborhood looking for her. Maybe, in a narcotic stupor, she had simply wandered away and was somewhere nearby. No luck.

At four that afternoon, the phone rang and Gwen answered it. It was Mom.

"Where are you?" Gwen, relieved but angry, demanded.

"Just listen to me. I need your help," Mom said. She sounded normal, lucid but a little frightened. "I'm in Atlanta . . ."

Richey had picked up the extension and interrupted. "Get your ass back home," he said.

Gwen, recognizing that she had no further part in the conversation, hung up. When Richey got off the phone, he told her that Mom was on her way back. The thought that formed in Gwen's mind was that Mom, needing to get away from Richey for a while, had slipped out of bed during the night, packed a bag and hit the road. She never found out what "help" Mom had wanted from her.

She talked to Richey about Mom's behavior, her work schedule, her drug use, about how everything seemed to be unraveling.

"She has got to stop this," she said.

Richey agreed. *Yes, something has to be done. We'll talk to her when she gets back. We'll take care of it.*

When Mom arrived, Gwen was braced for another confrontation, an argument over her need for treatment and her need for rest.

Richey acted as though nothing had happened. He just looked at Mom and handed her some papers. "Honey," he said, "you need to sign these."

Gwen was livid. After Mom had gone to the bedroom, she got in Richey's face and said, "You son-of-a-bitch, all you care about is her signing those papers."

She gathered her belongings and left the house, and her job. After that, Gwen moved out of the Tammy Wynette orbit. She'd had enough. It was too frustrating to be so close to someone she loved and have to stand by—helpless to do anything—while the situation continued to deteriorate.

She wasn't the only one who felt that Richey was pushing Mom too hard, using drugs to get her through shows that never should have been booked.

Jan Smith saw it, too. At an outdoor music festival in West Virginia, Mom was scheduled to close the show but during the day she became deathly sick. It was very hot and Mom was lying in bed, her skin so colorless that Jan thought she was going to die.

She got on the two-way radio and located Sue Richards, a backup singer, and asked her to come to the bus and help with Mom, who was getting sicker by the minute. They begged Richey to take Mom to the hospital, but he refused.

Mom got up and went into the bathroom and in a minute or two, Jan heard her scream and ran to her aid. When she opened the bathroom door, Mom was bent over the commode vomiting and excreting a thick black liquid.

Richey came back inside and said, "Clean her up."

Mom went on that night, but, mercifully, the show was cut short when somebody in the crowd tossed a handful of firecrackers onto the stage.

EVELYN SHRIVER HAD come to Nashville as a publicist for Randy Travis and soon began working for Mom, who toured with Randy for several years. In the early days, she was taken by the fun times and friendships that formed on those tours. She had seen Mom in her spunkier years.

She has told me about one Christmas when Mom and Randy were taping a special and got into a ruckus with the director, who wanted Randy to do something that didn't work very well. He began yelling at Randy, "We'll do it my way or no way."

Mom, in high heels and a red and white Christmas sweater, ran onto the set and pointed her finger a few inches from the director's face.

"Listen," she said, "you don't know what the hell you're doing. I've been working with you for twenty years and you've been a hack the whole twenty."

The guy blinked but was otherwise immobilized by the sudden assault. Mom seldom roared and no one on the set expected this.

"You start treating Randy right," she went on, "or we're all walking off this show and you can figure out what the hell you're going to do."

After that, Evelyn said, Randy was treated like royalty.

That was a long time ago. Evelyn was around long enough to watch illness and physical deterioration become a part of Mom's life, as she declined to the point that she would be unhooked from feeding tubes just seconds before walking on stage, nearly unable to breathe after singing one song.

In New York once, Mom got sick just before she was to appear on the Jay Leno show with George Jones. Richey's insistence that she make the appearance in spite of being sick infuriated Evelyn enough to make a scene that forced him to relent.

Evelyn dropped by the house one day and Mom was sitting on the sofa with an oxygen tank beside her. Her legs and feet were swollen and her skin was creased and ashen. Evelyn tried to conceal her concern, but obviously failed.

"Don't look so scared," Mom said. "I'm not going to die."

Evelyn had argued with Richey when Mom left on one of her European tours. She felt strongly that Mom should not go. "I believed she was going to come back in a coffin," she later told me.

She called Richey and pleaded with him to cancel the tour.

"She can't go," she argued. "She's going to die over there."

"Angel, we can't cancel," Richey said.

"Don't you understand?" Evelyn snapped. "You're working this woman to death. People look at Tammy and their hearts break that you keep her out on stage. They think it's all greed . . . for you to make money."

Richey began to cry.

"Angel, you know how much I love her. She's my whole life," he said.

"Then why are you doing this to her?" Evelyn pressed. "This is going to kill her."

"No it isn't," he said. "This is what keeps her alive."

"I don't agree with you, Richey, and I think it's wrong," Evelyn said.

"I would never do anything to hurt her."

Her lobbying failed, but she called Georgette and me and urged us to intervene to get Mom off the road for a while, to get her at home where she could rest and follow a proper diet. Again, though, there was nothing we could do. Tammy Wynette was not our ward.

After the European trip, Mom came home and had a long period to rest. Evelyn had hoped that she would use the time to exercise—maybe hire a personal trainer—and eat the kinds of foods that would not aggravate her intestinal maladies. Instead, as Evelyn described it, she seemed to collapse in on herself, to sink lower in the absence of a purpose, a reason to get out of bed and get dressed.

One day, Evelyn asked her, "Tammy, how can you go out and sing when you're barely able to talk?"

"I don't know," Mom said. "I just hold everything in for the performance. That's where I pour it all out."

Evelyn began to believe that perhaps Richey was correct, that Mom needed the spotlight and the applause to keep her going. My mother was driven to the heights she had scaled and driven to remain there. The show is just another narcotic, and just as dangerous.

JUST AFTER CHRISTMAS in 1993, Mom got sick in the middle of the night and it was bad enough that Richey rushed her to Baptist Hospital and sent a plane to Pittsburgh, where Dr. Marsh was now practicing, to bring him to Nashville. My sisters and I were notified early that morning, a few hours after Mom was admitted.

When I got to the hospital, she was as close to death, I suppose, as one can get and still be clinically alive. It was another blockage of the bile duct, and a shunt had to be installed to drain the infection. She was so bloated that she appeared to weigh twice her 110 pounds. Her blood pressure was thirty over something in the teens, according to Georgette, and it had bottomed out. She was being given Dopamine and Exedrene but her blood pressure was not responding. Her kidneys had shut down and other bodily functions were following suit. Her breath was so shallow that it barely provided life-sustaining oxygen to her heart.

When Georgette arrived from Alabama, she was visibly shaken, and since she is a nurse, her reaction scared me stiff. Our mother was receiving amounts of medication that approached the maximum the body can handle without the risk of kidney damage.

Evelyn Shriver showed up, prepared to write the obituary. The doctors had concluded that her abdomen was such a knot of scar tissue that further surgery would be futile. She was in a coma, or in and out of one, and basically was being kept alive by machines and tubes.

For five days, we waited and watched, rotating in and out in shifts. Many of her old friends came by, but she showed no signs of recognition. Richey had a suite next to her room and I don't think he ever left the hospital. The press had been following the story daily, and Richey seemed determined to conceal the seriousness of the situation.

"When you leave here," he warned me and my sisters, "don't talk to anyone about your mother's condition."

One day, I walked into his suite and caught him on the telephone with someone from the *Crook & Chase Show,* a popular TNN feature that focused on country-music stars. He was calling people and giving them daily updates.

Mom's condition showed little change for five days and we started to believe that each hour would be her last. Suddenly, the drugs began to work, her blood pressure made a tentative move toward normalcy, and she came out of the coma.

Encouraged, the doctors reconsidered the surgery option.

"We're going to give it one last try," Marsh told us. "If it doesn't work, she'll be dead by morning."

It would be a delicate procedure, requiring the precise removal of just the right scar tissue. The odds were not great, but neither was the alternative. If they didn't operate, she would probably die anyway.

We waited for hours for the doctors to come out and tell us the operation was a success, the blockage had been removed with no collateral damage.

Normally, an ordeal like the one she had just been through requires a lengthy recovery, a month or more for rest and follow-up tests. Three days after she was released from the hospital early in January, Mom was back on tour. Her first stop was somewhere in New England and she barely got through three songs before she broke into tears and had to call it quits. Later, she told Georgette that as she left the stage, all she could think about was how disappointed the audience would be and how amazed she was to discover that those fears had been sorely misplaced. As she was led to a chair in the wings, she received a standing ovation.

Sometimes, she tried to make light of her brush with death. Describing to Loretta Lynn the five days of floating in and out of coma, she said the room was mostly permeated with blurred faces and slurred voices. But she had a vague memory of one familiar face.

When she came to, she told Loretta, she asked Richey, "Did I see George Jones in my room while I was sick?"

He said, "Yeah, you did."

Mom said, "Oh God, I've already been to hell and back one time. I didn't want to go again."

Levity may have helped her maintain an illusion of composure, but I believe that near-death experience had a profound effect on her. She could no longer dismiss her medical problems as *just a part of my life.* The face of the reaper was now real to her and it was a face she could not easily put out of her mind.

"I remember seeing all my girls standing at the foot of my bed with tears in their eyes, and thinking, *That is a pretty picture,*" she told one interviewer. "I had no pain. I wasn't scared. It was all just very peaceful. I felt like I was floating somewhere. Maybe this is God's way of telling me that death ain't no big deal."

No big deal, perhaps, but still something she thought about often after that.

Eighteen

IF NEARLY DYING had a beneficial fallout, it was that my mother quit smoking, her habit of thirty years. It wasn't a conscious decision, she always said, but when she left the hospital she simply had no more craving for nicotine. As a result, she believed, her voice was stronger and clearer and she was ready once again to test her musical range.

Before that perilous hospital stay, she had recorded an album, *Honky Tonk Angels,* with Dolly Parton and Loretta Lynn, and it was considered something of a country-music landmark, a collection of pure barroom ballads by the three reigning jukebox queens.

Then, her legs feeling steadier and her voice stronger, she took on a different project, one that probably thrilled her as much as anything she had ever done. It was an album aptly titled *Without Walls* and she personally assembled an unlikely collection of voices and styles to pull it off. She sang with Elton John, Wynonna, Aaron Neville, Sting, Joe Diffie, Lyle Lovett, Cliff Richard and Smoky

Robinson. In a lot of duets, the singers do not sing together, but their tracks are recorded separately and combined electronically by the studio engineers. For this one, Mom insisted on being with each of her partners when they recorded.

That same year, she teamed up with George Jones to re-record "Golden Ring" for one of his albums and she made a guest appearance on the television show *Evening Shade,* which starred Burt Reynolds.

But her biggest triumph of the post-near-death months was an appearance at Carnegie Hall for Sting's annual Rainforest Foundation Benefit. Whitney Houston also performed and so did Pavarotti, Elton John, James Taylor, Aaron Neville and Branford Marsalis.

As I have said, I went through most of my life not really appreciating my mother's stature in the entertainment business. Seeing her in *Who's Who* when I was in high school had opened my eyes a little, but watching that rain forest benefit was the clincher.

Georgette was also moved by that event and, like me, derived from it a new perspective on the woman we called "Mom."

"It blew me away," Georgette said.

Our mother was in major-league company that night and it amazed us when James Taylor said, "It is the lifelong dream of all the performers here to share a stage with Tammy Wynette." It also did not escape our notice that she received the only standing ovation of the evening. Even *Rolling Stone* noticed Tammy Wynette "got the most thunderous ovation of the evening."

Given all that, I wondered why her life off stage was so troubled. She was now fifty years old and no longer a consistent chart-topper and Grammy winner, but those should have been golden years for Tammy Wynette, the elder stateswoman years, the doting grandmother years. Instead, she was on a frightening downward spiral.

Richey, too, was showing less and less inclination to help his wife whip her addiction. Once, they arrived in London for a show and discovered that they did not have Mom's painkillers with them. While she went to rehearsal, Richey got on the Concorde and made a quick round trip to New York for a fresh supply of narcotics.

In some ways, his personality was changing. Where he had been cleverly manipulative and controlling, he turned ugly and verbally abusive. They went to New York, where she was to be on the *Today* show and sing a song, "It's a Girl Thing," that Elton John got to her. Just before she was to walk on the set, Richey said, "Your hair looks like shit. You look like crap." She nearly cried. Why would he upset her just before an appearance on live, national television? No one around Tammy could figure it out, but several of those who traveled with them said it became almost standard for him to humiliate her and assault her confidence before a show.

Clearly, it was time to start drawing some lines, to cut down the number of personal appearances, to address the painkiller problem. Physically, Mom had changed so dramatically that old friends recoiled at the sight of her and rumors began to circulate around Nashville that she was afflicted with AIDS. But the beat went on.

When she was sick, she was whisked off to Pittsburgh and the care of Dr. Marsh, who, by then, was more than her doctor. He sometimes attended her concerts and music-industry events and became a friend. Because he was a distinguished liver-transplant specialist, rumors began to circulate that Mom was suffering from more than just intestinal blockages and adhesions.

One of the supermarket tabloids even published a story alleging that she was awaiting a liver transplant—a revelation that, if true, could have been devastating to her career.

She and Richey filed a lawsuit, which was settled out of court. Because the settlement documents were sealed, I never knew the exact amount they received, but I believe it was substantial.

Still, her frequent trips to Pittsburgh kept the rumor mill humming. If Marsh had been treating her for liver failure, it probably would have been no worse than what was actually happening.

Her need for intravenous feeding and sedation became so acute that a catheter was attached to her side to receive the injections. No more shots between the toes, no more searching for a functional vein. The needle was simply inserted into the catheter, which fed directly into her bloodstream.

To some of us, Georgette in particular, that was a disturbing landmark. It signaled a permanence to a condition that we were not ready to accept. Georgette had learned in nursing school that narcotics can cause bowel obstructions—one of Mom's frequent medical complaints—but we didn't know exactly what medications she was receiving. We had heard about the Demerol and the Dilaudid and we suspected other opiates were being administered. Surprisingly, Mom didn't seem to know much about her own condition or medications; she often asked Georgette to explain certain symptoms or drug reactions to her.

So we pressed Richey for information and he assured us that Dr. Marsh was contacting all of Mom's previous physicians and was compiling her complete medical history into a booklet. Each of her daughters would get a copy, he said, so we would know exactly where she stood. If that history ever *was* assembled, none of us received the promised copies.

Most of our questions were met with evasive answers by Richey and we were reluctant to press too hard. We believed that our mother's doctor would have her best interests at heart. We wanted to believe the same about Richey. Gwen and I had left home soon after he married our mother, and Tina left not far behind. Georgette, though, had pretty much grown up in the house with Richey and he had served as a father to her. She was not close to Jones in those days, and as a bride in 1989, it was Richey who gave her away.

We didn't like what was happening to our mother and we were a little confused, I guess. We didn't know who or what to blame. It was as though events were pre-ordained and everyone close to Tammy Wynette was compelled to ride along, powerless to effect change. We could only watch as the portable catheter was moved, as each location was exploited, from her side to her abdomen to her back. We knew that the device not only fed her addiction but carried another potentially lethal risk: a blood clot.

In November of 1996, Euple Byrd, Mom's first husband and father to Gwen, Tina and me, was killed in a car wreck. We were having a wedding party for Richey's son, Kelly, that night and Tina wasn't there. The phone call bearing the news came from her, which seemed fitting in a way. After Mom divorced him, Dad pretty much removed himself from our lives. He married again and divorced again and stayed away from us until Gwen was finishing high school. He came to her graduation and tried to

reestablish a relationship with us. We all welcomed the
gesture, and so did Mom, but of the three daughters, Tina
became closest to him.

That night Tina called to tell us that Dad was driving
home in the rain from a flea market when another car
crossed the center line and slammed into him head-on. The
woman driving the other car and her daughter were also
killed.

Mom was probably as upset as any of us. She and Dad
had become friends again. He often stayed at our house
when he came to Nashville to visit.

If her own health problems had not put thoughts of mor-
tality into her mind, Dad's sudden death certainly did.
Mom called all of us girls together the night he died and,
for the first time that I can remember, talked to us about
dying. She had prepared a will, she told us, that would provide for us in the event of her death. She owned two large
life insurance policies; one would go to Richey, the other
to us. Her will, she said, provided for her estate to be
placed in a trust, to be administered by Richey. When he
died, it would pass to her four children and his two.

There was a provision in the will that she said was very
important to her but seemed almost irrelevant to my sisters
and me. That provision was that if any one of the heirs
challenged the will, they would lose their inheritance. After Conway Twitty died, his children and widow got into a
prolonged battle that was trotted through the newspapers,
and Mom thought that was terrible—the family being
ripped apart in public over the fruits of a dead man's labor.
She wanted to make certain that didn't happen to us, and I
respected her for that.

She showed us a list, written on a yellow legal pad, of
personal items—clothing and jewelry and the like—that

she wanted each of us to have. We were uncomfortable talking about those things. Although we were aware of her precarious health, her death was not something we had allowed ourselves to contemplate. She was only fifty-three years old, after all.

I remember saying, "Mom, why are we talking about this? You're not going to die."

She laughed—an uneasy, self-conscious laugh—and said, "Someday I will . . . not anytime soon, I hope."

After that, when one of the daughters was at her house, she would pull out her legal pad and add to the list. It was a large house packed with things she had brought back from her travels all over the world. She had a set of China from England that she said she wanted me to have, so she put that on the list.

"Mom, this is morbid," I protested.

"Don't be embarrassed . . . don't be ashamed," she said. "Tell me what else you want."

Sorting through her jewelry one day, she was designating certain items for each daughter. I was uncomfortable and wanted to halt what I thought was a macabre inventory.

"Mom, when you die, I think you should be buried with your jewelry on," I told her.

"No," she said. "I want everybody to have something."

PHYLLIS HILL HAD worked in the country-music business for thirty years, the last fifteen of them doing research, footage clearance and other production tasks for The Nashville Network. In the summer of 1997, she had friends from Ireland who were visiting in her home and one of them, a singer named Margo O'Donnell, insisted on going to the Grand Ole Opry "to see Tammy."

Mom was scheduled to be on that portion of the Opry that is broadcast live, so Phyllis arranged to take her guests backstage. When they saw Mom, Margo gasped, "My God, something's wrong."

This was not the Tammy Wynette she had seen on television and in videos. This was a woman nearly in tears, nervous, distraught, unable to keep her earrings on or to button her clothes properly. Various attendants were buzzing around her, adjusting and primping her, but they couldn't make the adjustment she really needed. They couldn't tame the beast that was eating at her insides.

"If I was George Richey," Phyllis whispered to her friend, "I would stop her from going on."

Mom was nearly too weak to stand and her steps were halting, but she made it to the center of the stage and sat down on a stool that had been placed there for her. Phyllis, as well as a lot of other people in the theater that night, could not help but notice that her jacket was buttoned crooked.

It was also obvious that she was too feeble to sing. Just a couple of lines into her first song—I think it was "Stand by Your Man"—Lorrie Morgan, who was hosting the show, saw that she was in trouble and walked on stage, stood beside her and made the number a duet, to let her own voice nourish the number, to give Mom a voice she did not possess that night.

For her second song, Jan Howard joined her on stage and repeated the charity. I don't think there had ever been an occasion when another singer had to carry Tammy Wynette through a show, but without Lorrie and Jan, that night would have been a disaster.

As soon as she was finished, Richey held her arm and escorted her straight to the back door and to her bus.

Margo was determined to meet her, so she followed them outside and knocked on the door of the bus. Richey opened the door.

"I'm Margo O'Donnell," the singer said. "Please tell Tammy I'm here. I'd like to say 'hi' to her."

Richey closed the door and then reopened it a few seconds later.

"She can't see anybody right now," he said. It looked to Margo that he had not even consulted with her.

Hazel Hall also attended that show. She had come to Nashville for a visit and, like everyone else who had not seen Mom in a while, was floored by Mom's appearance. The afternoon before the show, she accompanied Mom to the beauty shop and afterward told her, "Now, let's ride around and talk."

Mom pulled into a little park by the river and turned off the ignition.

"I'm worried," Hazel said.

"What about?"

"The girls."

Mom said, "Why are you worried about them?"

"Tammy," Hazel said, "I know that you have been at the point of death several times. Now, honey, I want to know if you've got anything to protect them . . . like a will."

She put her hand on Hazel's knee and said, "Now, don't you worry about it. I've got an airtight will. I have a two-million-dollar policy. Richey is to get one million and the girls are to get the other, divided four ways."

"Are you sure?"

"Yes."

"Well, you know and I know that Richey doesn't care for your girls," Hazel said.

"You stinker," Mom said jokingly. "You know everything about me, don't you?"

"Just about," Hazel said.

"Well, don't worry. I've told them they could get all of my clothes and all of my jewelry."

SOMETIME AFTER THANKSGIVING that year, Mom seemed to understand the grim depths of her health problems and I think the premonition of death was standing larger than ever before her. Her old childhood friend Linda Cayson came to Nashville shortly before Christmas and was shocked by Mom's physical condition. She had aged years in the months since Linda had last seen her and she was sick once again with abdominal pains and nausea. More disturbing to Linda was her insistence on talking about death.

"Oh, hush," Linda said when Mom brought up the subject of dying. "I don't want to hear about that."

"Lin, I need to talk about it."

"Okay," Linda said when she realized Mom would not drop the subject. "*You* talk."

"You're not going to feel bad if they don't bring me back down to where Mother is buried, are you?"

"Lord, no, but you're not going to die. . . ."

"Yes I am, but I've lived here so long, my kids are here . . . I think I should be buried here," Mom said.

She seemed so certain of her fate that Linda suspected she knew more than she was telling. She was so emaciated that Linda made a logical guess.

"Tammy, do you have cancer?" she asked.

Mom kind of chuckled, but her response was revealing

because it suggested her own doubt that she was being told everything about her medical condition.

"Well, if I do, they haven't told me. I just hurt all the time," she said.

Linda wanted to talk about something else, but Mom seemed to be benefiting from getting her fears off her chest.

"Do you have everything in order . . . you know . . . legal papers, financial arrangements?" Linda asked.

"Oh, yes," Mom said. "The main thing is I want my daughters to be taken care of. I've got two one-million-dollar life insurance policies. One is made out to Richey and the other is for the girls. Then, when Richey is gone, everything will go to those kids."

Linda studied her face. She was fifty-five years old and looked eighty, Linda thought. Her fingers were pale and bony. The portable catheter bulged under her clothes.

Linda cried when she left to return home. She was certain she would never see my mother again.

"I expect to hear anytime that she is gone," she told her own daughters a couple of days later.

GWEN WASN'T AROUND a lot at the end. Unwilling to watch the painful spectacle of her mother's decline, and frustrated by the futility of it all, Gwen had drifted away.

"It's like sitting and watching Mom kill herself," Gwen told me, and I wholeheartedly agreed. It seemed that every conversation with our mother was a heart stopper.

Once, after Mom hadn't seen Gwen for a while, she called.

They talked for a few minutes and Gwen had an uneasy sense that there was a reason for the call.

"Is anything wrong?" Gwen asked her.

"Well . . . I've found a lump in my breast. I've got to have a biopsy and . . . I may need surgery."

What do you say at a time like that? Gwen tried to console her and assure her that it was probably nothing serious, that a lot of women have breast lumps that turn out to be harmless tissue.

"I know," Mom said. "But I just wanted to say I love you."

"I love you, too," Gwen said.

The lump was benign, thank God, but the constant dread of her health problems was hard to live with.

In 1997, after our father's death, Gwen was handling his estate and Mom disagreed with something she was doing. They had an argument and Gwen didn't talk to her for a long time after that.

I, too, found myself avoiding the Wynette household. Even her old friends didn't come around much anymore. Martha Dettwiller tried to stay in touch, as did Jan Smith and Nanette Crafton, but it wasn't easy. Some days, Mom would be so out of it that she couldn't even talk on the phone. Other days, she would be romping around the house like a teenager. No one ever knew what to expect.

Once, after seeing her on a particularly good day, Martha called and suggested they go to lunch and do some shopping. Mom's mood had already turned down. She talked about how bad she looked and said, "I don't want people to see me like this."

Therefore, we all were encouraged when, late in March, she went to work planning a baby shower for Karen Sloas, one of her backup singers. It seemed to give her a sense of purpose and a renewed vitality, and Mom insisted on doing just about everything herself: the invitations, the shopping, the cooking and the decorating. It was one of the happiest times I had spent with her in a long, long time and I went home afterward thinking that maybe I had become too morose about her condition and too pessimistic about her chances of salvaging her life.

For a few springtime, sunlit hours, her effusiveness masked her frailty and she was her old self again, the bubbly hostess, the extravagant entertainer. She laughed and played the way she had when Gwen and I were young and our friends filled the house on the Saturday afternoons that she could be with us. She was *just Mom* again.

The next week she was dead.

PART THREE

Blood Secrets

Nineteen

AFTER THE FUNERAL, I found myself brooding much more than I normally do. I had been upset the night Mom died, enraged by the scene inside her house and distressed by a sequence of events that made no sense to me. Newspapers and television stations had carried the standard obituaries and tributes that recounted her life and her journey across the world stages, and each account spoke of her passing as a tragic loss for country music and the fans who adored her. Not one account that I saw, however, made note of anything peculiar about the circumstances surrounding her death. But then, why should they? In those first hours and days, the reporters knew less than I, which wasn't much.

I had a tote bag full of questions, but no one to whom I could address them. What time did she die? Why did she die? Who was there? Why was a local doctor not called? What had occurred in the hours preceding her death? How did the *National Enquirer* hear about it before her daughters? Why did Richey call his lawyer when he had not called an ambulance? Why did Dr. Marsh make it a point to tell me that all her vital signs had been good and that she was gaining weight? How did he know that? When was the last time he examined her? Most important, why did he say that the cause of death was a blood clot—something he could not have known for certain?

What preyed on me was the idea that somehow someone had screwed up and my mother had died as a result of it. Even if there had been no error, no negligence, I still wanted the truth.

My sisters shared my bewilderment, but with the exception of Tina, we had been afraid to put our thoughts into words, to wonder aloud what really happened. We talked to each other. We talked to Mom's closest friends. We tried to believe that we were letting our grief rule our intellect, that we were seeing boogeymen where there were only shadows of sorrow. Yet the troubling, unanswered questions kept accumulating.

Two days after the funeral, I ran into an old friend, who hugged me and expressed her condolences and then asked, "What's going on?"

"What do you mean?" I asked.

"I heard something on *Geraldo Rivera* last night . . . something about Tammy Wynette's daughters being suspicious about her death."

I'm always amazed at how few secrets the family of a celebrity can have. From time to time, I had talked to reporters, even tabloid reporters, and I didn't always resent what I considered their invasions of our lives, but I often wondered how family matters could get on the street so quickly. This time, I was put off by my suspicions making national television so soon after Mom's death. For one thing, I did not want to accuse anyone of anything. I just wanted answers, information, some rational account of my mother's last hours. It did not seem that alienating those close to her was the best way to tap their candor.

There had been no open hostility between Richey and me or between him and Gwen or Georgette, so far as I knew. Tina had been pretty outspoken about her feelings but she had not confronted Richey with them. And Gwen had actually maintained a surprising level of civility toward him. They had had their battles in the past, but she was able to discount those and do what she felt was necessary to get through a difficult time. Gwen checked in on him daily after the funeral to help him with whatever details she could handle. Each of us was trying to give him and Dr. Marsh the benefit of every doubt we had.

IN MID-MAY, A meeting was called in the office of the attorney who was handling Mom's will and her estate. There were six of us present—Gwen, Tina, Georgette, Deirdre, Kelly and me. Richey was not present. The purpose of the meeting was to go over the will and to brief us on its provisions.

The attorney gave each of us a copy, which we did not read thoroughly at the time. We skimmed through it, while he related the highlights to us. He explained that Richey and his brother Carl would serve as cofiduciaries of the will and the estate or, if one was deceased or unable to serve in that capacity for some reason, Sylvia Richardson would be the co-executrix. That was the first flag to go up. Mom knew that her daughters did not have a cozy relationship with Richey and she had acknowledged to Hazel Hall that she was aware that Richey did not care for us. Yet her will gave Richey and his family—even an ex–sister-in-law—dominion over our interests in her estate. Could there not have been a co-executor from her side of the family, someone in whom her daughters would have placed more trust? Sure. It seemed peculiar that she did not do that.

The attorney skimmed quickly over parts pertaining to the disposition of debts, business property and artistic and creative assets—such as royalties—and then to what seemed most pertinent to Mom's and Richey's children:

> *I may prepare a written memorandum listing certain items of tangible personal property which I wish certain persons to have. I request that my wishes, as set forth in any such memorandum, be observed. If no such memorandum shall be found with this will, then it shall be presumed that none exists and all of my tangible personal property shall pass as provided in the remainder of this article.*

Certainly such memorandum existed. We had seen it often in the past year and a half.

> *I give and bequeath the sum of ten thousand dollars to each grandchild of mine living at my death and a like sum to each grandchild of my said husband living at the time of my death. In the case of any such grandchild who has not attained the age of twenty-three years, the bequest for such grandchild shall be distributed to a parent or guardian of such grandchild, as selected by my executor or trustee, the same to be held in trust for the use and benefit of such grandchild until . . . the age of twenty-three. While such funds are being held for such grandchild,*

the income and principal thereof may be used for the
health and educational needs of such grandchild as
determined in the sole discretion of the trustee hold-
ing the funds.

None of her grandchildren was of the designated age,
so Richey and his brother would retain control of that
money, too.

We did not find it unusual that Mom bequeathed no sum
of money to any of her children. She told us she had handled that through the two million-dollar life insurance policies. The proceeds of one would go to Richey. The other
would be divided among Gwen, Tina, Georgette and me.
She had told us that in Richey's presence. If it wasn't true,
why didn't he correct her?

As the attorney explained the next couple of pages—basically that Richey was to receive the house on Franklin
Road and all personal property and control over her business and professional assets—I could see Tina's lips tight-
ening and her eyes narrowing.

There was something about a George B. Richardson
Marital Trust and a Virginia W. Richardson Family Trust
and a Virginia W. Richardson Special Trust, all of which
would be controlled by Richey and Carl or, in the alternative, Sylvia. For example:

For so long as my husband, George B. Richard-
son, shall survive me . . . Trustee shall collect the in-
come and profits from the property comprising the
Virginia W. Richardson Family Trust and shall accu-
mulate or distribute, at any time and from time to
time, so much of the net income therefrom as Trustee,

*in the exercise of Trustee's sole and absolute discre-
tion, may deem advisable to provide for the health,
maintenance, education and support of my said husband; any of the income and profits of the trust estate
not distributed to my said husband may be paid and
distributed by Trustee in such amounts and propor-
tions as Trustee . . . without regard to equality of dis-
tribution, may deem advisable to provide for the
health, maintenance, education and support of any
one or more of the following persons: My living children; the living children of my said husband; the living issue of any deceased child of mine (and of) my
said husband.*

Because the will did not request it, no inventory of her
estate would be made, we were told, and, therefore, we
would have no idea of its contents or value. We knew the
house was worth nearly a million dollars, that her tour
buses were probably worth half a million and that she
owned property in Alabama that was worth something. We
believed that the settlement of the lawsuit over the erro-
neous liver transplant story had put a substantial amount in
her bank account. Beyond that, we knew very little. We assumed that her music was still generating healthy royalties,
but we did not have access to the precise numbers. That
was all Richey's business now.

Then we received the surprising news that the will being read to us was not the original will that Mom signed. It
was a copy, one that the lawyer assured us was genuine,
authentic and accurate.

Was he telling us that Mom's will had been misplaced?
It just couldn't be located, we were told.

What about the memorandum mentioned in the will, the

list of personal items and how they were to be distributed? No such list had been found, we were told.

Tina had heard enough. She got up and walked out of the meeting.

Richey had asked us to come by his house after the meeting and we had no idea why. But when we got there, each of us was given an affidavit to sign. It stated that we accepted the copy of the will as authentic. Maybe we were confused by the legalese of all this, I don't remember. Maybe we were remembering Mom's intent that her will not be challenged and the family not engage in warfare over whatever she left behind, I don't know.

We had our suspicions and our questions about our mother's death, but at the time we had no thought of taking legal action. We signed the affidavits.

All except Tina. "This is not what Mom wanted," she had said when she left the lawyer's office. She did not bother to make the pilgrimage to Richey's house.

Eventually, Richey gave each of us—excluding Tina—$5,000 and, frankly, I was appreciative. He was not required to do it, and I took it as a gesture of kindness, an advance against the money from the life-insurance policy we would receive later.

Gwen was so touched that she began crying. "You don't have to do this," she told Richey.

GWEN WONDERED ABOUT the frequent phone calls from Sheila Slaughter. We knew her slightly. Sheila was thirty-two years old and had once been a Dallas Cowboys cheerleader. She was also a television producer and had worked on a program about Mom, so I assume that was how they met. I never had the impression that they were chummy.

Now, within days of the funeral, she was calling the house so often that within a month Gwen sensed this woman was more than one of Mom's casual friends.

Sometimes, after her calls, Richey would cancel dinner plans and disappear. One night, she called after eleven o'clock and Richey left soon afterward, telling Gwen, "I'm going over to Sheila's house."

Frequently Gwen and Tina drove by the Richeys' and saw Sheila's car there—late at night, early morning, it didn't matter.

Finally, Gwen asked him about what seemed to be a new woman in his life so soon after his wife's death.

"Honey, she's just a friend," Richey said. "She's trying to help me get over the pain of losing your mom."

He wasn't wholly convincing, but because he was nearly twice Sheila's age, his explanation was not without a whiff of credibility.

It wasn't until we found out about the life-insurance policy that we began to believe that we had been naive in thinking that the wishes Mom had often expressed to us would be carried out. Of course, the legal pad on which she had itemized the personal possessions each of us was to receive never turned up, so we got nothing. Then we discovered that we were not, as Mom had told us, named as beneficiaries on one of her insurance policies.

One of the policies listed Richey as a beneficiary, but proceeds of the other were to go to "the estate of the insured." That was absolutely contrary to what Mom had been telling us and what she had told Hazel Hall and Linda Cayson.

The documents we saw indicated that a $1 million policy, No. 58090713, had been issued in July 1988 by the

Manufacturers Life Insurance Company to "Virginia W. Richey." The beneficiary: "The estate of the insured."

Line 3J on the application for the policy asks the question: *Will this policy replace any life insurance or annuity policy on the life insured, or owned by the Owner?*

The box was checked "Yes."

If yes, give company and policy number.

Written in the blank reserved for the policy being replaced was: *Manulife #3032294-S.*

We never received any information about the previous policy, the amount or the beneficiaries. Because we had no reason to doubt what Mom had told us, we could only speculate that an existing policy had been changed for some reason at some point in time.

In September, just two months later, the same insurance company issued another million-dollar policy to "Virginia W. Richey." The beneficiary was "George W. Richey."

To my knowledge, Mom had never used the name "Richey" on any official or legal documents. It was not her legal name.

At any rate, what all of this meant to us was simple: We would not receive any money from the insurance company and we would receive only the personal items that Richey saw fit to give us.

Gwen questioned Richey about the insurance and all he would tell her was, "Your Mom changed that because she didn't want you to get it all at once."

For the most part, I had remained silent, marking time to see what Richey would do, waiting to see if he would carry out any of the things Mom led us to expect. But that didn't happen.

In July, about the time Gwen stopped her daily visits to

the house, I called Richey and told him I wanted to come by and talk with him. As always, it felt strange in the house. I had been by often since Mom died, and each time I was struck by a sensation of treading on alien ground; it just didn't feel like home anymore. Most of the family pictures she treasured had been removed and there was little of her left there . . . except the smell. Every time I walked in, I could still smell her.

I sat down in Richey's office and asked what we could expect from our mother's estate.

"I'm going to do exactly what your mom wanted done," he said. "I intend to promote her memory."

Richey could be very persuasive. I've often told people that I could walk into the room in a red dress and before I left he could have me believing it was blue. I was still susceptible to his wiles, but my naivete was fading fast.

"What are you going to do?" I asked him.

"I intend to give you girls what your mother wanted," he said. "I have to wait till September [the deadline for claims to be filed against the estate]. After that, Carl and I will decide what we want to do . . . how much money we want to give you girls. We don't want to give you all the money at one time. Tammy changed her mind about that."

Just like that. Tammy changed her mind. Carl and I will decide how much to give you. I was having a hard time holding my temper.

"Well," I said, calmly and probably a little icily, "Mom intended for the money to be used for us to buy a home . . . can you buy me a home, or can the estate buy me a home?"

He realized I was challenging him.

"Well, if I do it for you, I'll have to do it for everybody," he said.

"Okay," I said. *Do it,* I was thinking. *Buy everybody a house.*

"We'll have to wait and see," he said.

If Mom had "changed her mind," as Richey said, why hadn't she told her daughters?

MY ANGER BUILT as I thought back to the years of my mother's life that were spent in abject addiction, to the nights she went on stage when she could barely walk or talk, to the physical decline of her last months, to the day of her death and the questions I had pushed to the back of my mind.

Richey had made a great public display of his sorrow, but it was belied by his behavior. With a great flourish, he announced that he would see to it that fresh flowers were placed at Mom's tomb every Monday. They stopped arriving after a couple of months.

We found out that in July, Richey and Sheila Slaughter had gone to Europe together. While he limped around Nashville, still outwardly grief-stricken over the loss of his wife, he had a blonde half his age in the shadows. My sisters and I discovered one day that the pictures and notes we had placed at Mom's tomb had disappeared. An attendant at the mausoleum told us that "a blond lady with a little dog" had taken them down.

Two weeks after Mom was buried, Richey wrote a letter to the *National Enquirer.* Actually, it was an open letter to the readers of the tabloid, thanking the "fans around the world for their outpouring of love and sympathy during this most difficult time." He wrote of her roles of wife, soul mate, mother, grandmother and First Lady of Country Music. "The immensity of our grief simply reflects the magnitude of our love for her."

Richey seemed to love the tabloids—and knew how to manipulate them. He knew the audiences they reached and the subtle effect they had on those who feed on the lives of celebrities.

By September, I was angry enough to fight him on that very turf.

Tina was already talking openly about her feelings. She had talked to a lawyer friend to see if there was legal action we could take and she had contacted Larry Brinton, who has a morning talk show on Channel Five in Nashville. It was time for me to speak out, too.

I talked to Jan Smith about going public with my thoughts and she suggested that I call her son, Cannon, who lived in California. Cannon gave me the name of a woman, Janet Charlton, who wrote for the *Star*. She and I corresponded a few times and she put me in touch with Roger Hitts, another writer for the *Star*. When I told him what I wanted to do, he was as excited as a kid at Christmas. This story would not require anonymous sources or quotes. No hedging, just Tammy Wynette's daughter unplugged and on the record. He wanted to meet as soon as possible.

The tabloids have reputations for reporting rumors as news, for being casual about their facts when it comes to stories on celebrities, for printing what sells. That didn't bother me. Richey had sought out the *Enquirer* to flaunt his grief after the funeral. Maybe the *Star* was the battlefield I was looking for.

Twenty

AFTER TALKING TO the *Star* writers in the middle of September, I sort of held my breath for several days. I was eager for the story to appear, but I was apprehensive that it would get into print before September 23, the night of the annual Country Music Association's awards show. Mom died without knowing it—Richey had hoped to surprise her—but she was going to be inducted into the CMA Hall of Fame that night, on a show broadcast live on CBS and on BBC radio.

Now she would join Elvis Presley and George Morgan in a posthumous induction. Plans had been made for all the children, Tammy's and Richey's, to assemble at his house and ride in the limousine to the Grand Ole Opry House. I wanted very much to be a part of that evening, but if the article appeared before the show, all of Tammy's daughters probably would have been frozen out. On the Thursday before the show, I checked for the *Star* at a supermarket and was relieved to see that the story wasn't there. We would all be able to get through Wednesday night without a brawl. I could make one last visit to my mother's house. After that, I didn't care what happened.

There was another reason I was pleased that the story did not appear that week. I had hired Martha Dettwiller's attorney, Doug Brown, to find out what was going on with the estate. The day before the awards show, Doug and I met with Richey and his brother Carl to talk about it.

Richey was very nervous, and when Doug asked him about the life-insurance policies—how many there were and the amounts—Richey at first refused to answer.

"I don't have to tell you that," he said to Doug.

"Yes, you do, because Jackie is an heir to the estate," Doug advised him.

Richey clenched his jaw and said nothing.

"So you can either tell us now or we'll find out later," Doug said.

Richey relented. He told us that he had received $1.4 million from the policy of which he was the beneficiary and $1 million from the policy designated for the estate.

What of that second policy, the one Tammy Wynette intended to benefit her daughters? Doug asked.

"That went to satisfy debts against the estate," Richey said.

"How much is the estate worth?" Doug said.

"I have no idea what it's worth," Richey said.

Assuming we had extracted all the information Richey would surrender at the moment, Doug and I left.

The next evening, we all gathered at Richey's house to ride together to the CMA awards. To say the air in the house was frosty would be an epic understatement. Everyone was mannerly but muted and the look on Richey's face seemed to echo a famous W. C. Fields line: *On the whole,*

I'd rather be in Philadelphia. When everyone was present and the small talk had dwindled to awkward silence, we piled into the limousine and started up the sloping driveway toward Franklin Road.

We had barely pulled away from the house when another limo came purring down the drive. Our driver had to stop and back up to let it pass.

We all turned to look back as the other limo stopped and a woman hopped out.

"Who's that?" Tina said.

It was a young blonde wearing a dress cut dangerously low in the back.

Gwen said, "It's Sheila."

Richey sat quietly, leaning back in his seat, never acknowledging that a woman was entering his house. My guess was that he and Sheila had arranged for her to stop by the house and pick up passes to the show. My guess also is that Richey had wanted her to wait until we were gone.

We saw Sheila later at the show, but she and Richey hardly acknowledged each other. For this night, he was the somber widower of the First Lady of Country Music.

It was easy enough for me to take my mind off both of them. The show was touching and nostalgic. George Jones was a winner again, for his "You Don't Seem to Miss Me" duet with Patty Loveless, and the Hall of Fame segment was inspired. *Mom would have loved this,* I kept thinking. Her old pal Randy Travis sang tributes to George Morgan, while Lorrie Morgan, George's daughter, teamed with Pam Tillis for tributes to Tammy Wynette. Salutes to Elvis were raised by Travis Tritt and Wynonna.

But lurking in the back of my mind was that *Star* interview. I knew it was going to kick up a lot of dust and that my informal association with Richey, tenuous as it had been, would be severed. What would the rest of Nashville think? I couldn't imagine. What would Mom's friends think? I had a pretty good idea.

THERE WERE BUTTERFLIES in my stomach when I picked up the *Star* the next day. Having your words and thoughts on paper for millions of people to read is intimidating. I wondered if I had done the right thing and wondered if the *Star* had accurately interpreted and reported what I said.

The headline stripped across the top of the magazine's cover said, TAMMY WYNETTE DEATH MYSTERY. Below it, in smaller type, were the words "Her kids demand autopsy."

Quickly, I turned to the inside. Pages six and seven opened to form a two-page spread with three pictures— one of Mom kissing me on the cheek, one of Mom by herself and one of Richey about to collapse at the Ryman memorial service. TAMMY WYNETTE'S KIDS DEMAND NEW PROBE OF HER DEATH, the headline read.

Leaping out from the page, in large bold type, were a few of the questions I had been asking: *Why did husband refuse to call 911? Why did will disappear? Where are her millions?*

My apprehensions began to melt as I read the story and my own words:

"First off, we were told she died around seven P.M. that day. But I think it was closer to five-thirty because it was already all over town and working its way onto the local news programs. But Richey didn't call 911 or any local medical people, he called my mom's doctor at the University of Pittsburgh, Wallis Marsh.

"Richey sent a plane for him, and he didn't arrive until around midnight. He told us she died of a blood clot in her lung. I don't know how you can tell just by looking at somebody how they died.

"Richey and Dr. Marsh didn't contact the coroner until well after midnight and her body wasn't removed from the house until two-thirty in the morning."

The story talked about the will and a little about my past relationship with Richey, then ended with more of my words:

"I would hope Richey gives me a reason to trust him—I wouldn't be taking my story to the *Star* if I trusted him the way that I should. But I thought somebody should speak out.

"Richey's been taken care of for the whole time he was married to my mom, and he will continue to be taken care of. But he's made things hard on all of us, since the moment she died."

The last paragraph raised the subject of an autopsy, which had not been mentioned publicly before. I told the reporters that Tina and I had checked into the legal issues and found that we were powerless.

"The legal right belongs to Richey alone, we can't force him to do it. But we hope he would, since he knows it is our wish."

Closing the magazine and staring at the cover again, I realized that the butterflies were gone. I was no longer anxious about the repercussions of the article. For better or worse, the pit was open and the devil was loose.

FOR TEN YEARS or more, I had carried in my gut the vague anticipation that someday, in the wee hours, I would get a phone call that my mother was dead. I always expected it would be the result of a drug overdose. If I had received that call, it would have been painful, but bearable. Martha Dettwiller and Nan Crafton and Jan Smith and God knows how many other of her friends felt the same way.

Five months after she died, I still could not accept the doctor's conclusion that she was killed by a blood clot to the lung. There was no doubt in my mind that drugs contributed to her death. Exactly how was the question.

Through a friend, Georgette had met private detective Bobbi Casper and we hired her to see what she could find in a search of public records.

Fairly quickly, she turned up two interesting pieces of information. The first was the death certificate, signed by Dr. Marsh.

Under *IMMEDIATE CAUSE,* Marsh had written, "Pulmonary Embolus."

Under *Conditions leading to immediate cause* were "Indwelling vena cava Catheter" and "Small Bowel Dismotility."

That was interesting because, first, the doctor could not definitively diagnose pulmonary embolus (blood clot) without an autopsy, and, second, if that was the cause, the catheter he prescribed could have led to it.

The *indwelling catheter* is a tube placed in the body's largest vein for the administration of drugs. One of the known risks of such a device is blood clotting. Small bowel dismotility is a known side effect of opiates such as Demerol and Dilaudid. All three items listed on the death certificate could be connected with the doctor's prescribing and treatment.

Another document the detective turned up was the "Report of Investigation by County Medical Examiner."

It listed the cause of death as *natural* and *not a medical examiner case.* On the next page, the medical examiner, who never visited the house that evening, listed the time of death as "7:00 P.M." and the discovery of the death as "7:00 P.M." It said the police were notified at "7:00 P.M." and the medical examiner was notified at "9:15 P.M." The space for *last seen alive* contained only two squiggly lines.

I knew immediately that at least one piece of that information was absolutely not right. Tammy Wynette did not die at seven o'clock. Reporters had heard of it about two hours earlier.

Bobbi also obtained a copy of the police report and it, too, contradicted the medical examiner's report—and it conflicted with something very important that we would learn later. On the police report, it states that the call concerning Tammy Wynette's death was received at "2030 hours." To those of us who don't use military time, that means eight-thirty in the evening.

In his report, Officer J. Fuqua wrote:

> Tonight at approximately 2030 hrs, I responded to 4916 Franklin Rd. where it was determined that . . . Tammy Wynette had passed away at her home from degenerative disease she had been battling for years. Victim had been asleep on the couch in the den most of the afternoon. At approx. 1900 hrs her husband and her housekeeper checked on her and victim was dead. Dr. Marsh was en route from Pittsburgh and would handle all legal process. The ME's office was notified and the body released to Woodlawn.

What degenerative disease? Who told him that?

A supplemental police report was written by Officer Sam Roberts and it indicated that he received a call at "22:30"—ten-thirty that same evening. From his report:

Victim was lying on a sofa in the center room of her residence. Med-Com on the scene. Med-Com check for any heart-rate activity. Victim's two daughters were at the scene, Tina Jones, Gwen Nichols, who stated victim was under the care of Dr. Wallis Marsh. Contacted Dr. Marsh by phone, his statement was Virginia Richardson illness was a small bowel dismotility—H/X DRT Pulmonary embolus. Medications were Cipro 500 mg, Caphalex 250 mg, Lovanox, Keflex, Flagyl 375. Virginia Richardson appeared to have been deceased several hours. According to her daughter, Mrs. Richardson was last seen by her nurse on this date around 12:00. C.I.D.—Medical examiner contacted.

The various times noted on the various reports just didn't add up. If, as the medical examiner stated, the police were notified at seven o'clock, why did one officer receive the call at eight-thirty and another report that he received it at ten-thirty?

What was more striking in that report was the term "pulmonary embolus." The officer's conversation with Dr. Marsh took place before Marsh left Pittsburgh. So, from more than five hundred miles away, Marsh had already diagnosed the cause of death as a blood clot to the lung.

But there was more.

The list of medications Dr. Marsh gave the officer contained only antibiotics and blood thinners. We all knew she was receiving large amounts of painkillers. Why did the doctor not reveal that? Why did none of the reports mention the catheter attached to my mother's back, through which she was fed and medicated? The police didn't look and the medical examiner was candid enough to note in his report, in the space allotted for *Description of body*: "Not Seen."

Nobody saw anything, nobody asked any questions.

THERE WAS ONE other critical piece of evidence still to arrive: a tape of the belated 911 call to the police.

I was convinced of certain facts: that my mother had been dead for hours, perhaps the entire day; and at some point during that day Richey made at least two phone calls, one to Dr. Marsh, more than five hundred miles away, and one to his lawyer, before Mom's daughters were notified. At least an hour and a half—and perhaps longer—had elapsed from the time Richey found the body to the time the lawyer called 911 at about nine minutes to nine. During that time, Mom's personal effects, including her medications, had been moved, even though they might have provided clues to the cause of Mom's death. The time of the 911 call also conflicts with the times noted on the police and medical examiner's reports.

This is a transcript of the 911 call:

Operator: "Emergency 911, Sherry."

Caller: "Yes . . . We've had a death at 4916 Franklin Road. Could you send someone, please."

Operator: "Okay. Was it an expected death, sir?"

Caller: "Uh, it was kind of unexpected, but it was a natural death, yes."

Operator: "Well, we have been getting several calls and I'm not going to put this over the radio. Is this, by any chance, Tammy Wynette?"

Caller: "Yes, it is."

Operator: "Okay, sir."

Besides calling people who knew Mom, the reporters

from the *National Enquirer* had also been calling the police department since before six o'clock.

In most cities, a high-profile death gets the immediate attention of the local medical examiner, even if trauma, foul play or suicide is not indicated. In my mother's case, the ME's office not only showed zero interest, it completed its report on her death without ever viewing the body, made no attempt to determine the time of death, entered questionable information in its report and allowed the body to be released to the mortuary and embalmed without anything more than a cursory inquiry.

In my interview with the *Star* I had not been emphatic about an exhumation and autopsy. In fact, that issue may have been raised by the writers. However it came up, it was worth only one paragraph at the end of the story. No more.

My sisters and I were determined to get to the bottom of the discrepancies in the various accounts of April 6, 1998.

Twenty-one

MY COMMENTS IN the *Star* provoked no response from Richey. Zilch. I didn't really expect him to call up in a rage and read me the riot act, but I expected something. As I have said, Richey can be very persuasive and it would not have surprised me if he had tried to convince me that my suspicions were misplaced and my anger misdirected.

But, I heard nothing. There may have been two reasons. The first was that Richey probably didn't want to provoke or prolong a fight with Tammy Wynette's daughters. She had been feisty and headstrong and, when she was truly angered, more of a hellcat than most people wanted to tangle with. We, after all, were our mother's daughters. Richey probably thought we would let off steam for a while and then everything would blow over. The second reason was that dealing with the headlines about his personal life may have been keeping him preoccupied.

A week after the *Star* article, another piece appeared in the tabloid *Globe*. The headline said: JUST 6 MONTHS AFTER

NASHVILLE QUEEN'S TRAGIC DEATH . . . TAMMY WYNETTE'S
HUBBY ROMANCING SEXY BLONDE.

One paragraph said:

> *Tammy's husband, George Richey, 62, collapsed*
> *with grief at a Nashville memorial service to her on*
> *April 9, sobbing, "I can't bear to live without you."*
> *But just six months later, he's cooing sweet nothings*
> *to a 32-year-old TV producer and ex–Dallas Cow-*
> *boys cheerleader Sheila Slaughter, say pals.*

The article also noted that Richey and Sheila had tried
to keep their romance "under wraps" and made "special efforts not to be photographed together" when they made the
trip to Europe in July, just three months after Mom's death.

It was getting harder and harder for Richey to maintain
the grieving-widower image. Since the cover had been
blown, Richey and Sheila decided to make their first public
appearance—their U.S.A debut, anyway—a couple of
weeks later. The event: a tribute to Tammy Wynette.

MIKE EDGAR, ONE of my coworkers at EuroTan, handed
me a flier and said, "I guess you're going to this."

I looked at it for a moment and couldn't believe what I
was seeing. It concerned a fund-raising event for the Ear
Foundation, a charity for the hearing-impaired, in the form
of a special tribute to my mother. Randy Travis, Wynonna
Judd and Tanya Tucker were the featured celebrities.

"Mike, you got this in the mail?" I said.

"Yeah."

"What is this about?"

"I figured you knew," he said.

I had not received an invitation and, in fact, had heard absolutely nothing about it. Neither had my sisters. The job of informing us probably had been left to Richey and there weren't many lines of communication left between us. We were fast reaching the point where we could communicate only through tabloid newspapers or lawyers.

If he thought we wouldn't find out about it, he obviously was wrong. If he thought that withholding an invitation would keep us away, he had not been paying attention for the past twenty years.

I got in touch with my sisters and three of us—Gwen was not available that night—agreed to attend the Ear Foundation shindig. The Berlin Wall couldn't have kept us out. To emphasize the presence of the Wynette clan, I took my daughters with me.

The evening was divided into two parts: a large party for warming up with drinks and fellowship and, later, a musical performance—the tribute to Mom—at the Ryman Auditorium.

We didn't learn until we got to the party that Richey and Sheila had selected this night for their "coming out." My face flushed and I felt a sting of adrenaline when I saw them, but I elected to ignore them and hoped they would reciprocate in kind. Like me, Georgette preferred to shun Richey rather than acknowledge him.

Tina . . . well, Tina is Tina, more like our mother and scrappier than the rest of us—and more obstinate. When we were young, Mom did not hesitate to paddle us when we misbehaved. Gwen and I would cry and yell when we were spanked, but Tina would just take it, grit her teeth and say, "I'm not gonna cry . . . I'm not gonna cry." That would make Mom angrier and she would spank harder. Gwen and I used to tell her, "Tina, just cry and it won't be as bad." All she would say is, "I'm not gonna cry."

Tina is tough. She was born prematurely and weighed only about two pounds at birth. She contracted spinal meningitis when she was four months old and, because she was small and had spent most of her life in an incubator, the doctors told Mom that her chances of surviving were slim. But she survived and that may have made her a little harder than her sisters.

At some point in the evening, Tina walked over to Richey and Sheila and pretty soon we could hear her voice rising above the gentle murmur of the schmoozing crowd. I wasn't close enough to hear what was being said, but from what others have told me, Tina began by telling them they were a disgrace.

"You're a hypocrite," she told Richey. "I see her car in the driveway at Mom's house, last thing at night and first thing in the morning, so she's sleeping over. You pretend you're heartbroken, but you're sleeping with Sheila."

Many of the guests were obviously uncomfortable watching a family squabble being played out in public. Brian Williams, president of the bank where Mom did business, found someone to break up the confrontation. You couldn't really call it an argument. Tina was doing all the talking while Richey and Sheila just stood there, looking like they wanted to be beamed up and out of the room. There wasn't much they could say or do, not with every ear in the place cocked and every eye on them.

As two guys in dark suits approached Tina with the assignment of escorting her away, I remember, I thought they might have to call for reinforcements. No. She went quietly. She had had her say.

I must have had a grim look on my face, but inside I was smiling from a special feeling for my younger sister. I was very proud of her.

NOTHING WAS HAPPENING. Aside from possibly making George Richey squirm a little, my public comments to the tabloids and Tina's public scolding of him and Sheila Slaughter had accomplished nothing. What did we expect? I'm not sure. We may have hoped that by pointing out the unusual events surrounding Mom's death we could induce someone in a position of authority to take an interest in the case.

It seemed to me that just a casual reading of the police and medical examiner's report would be enough to do that. Woman dies. Emergency 911 not called for two hours. Cause of death diagnosed by telephone. Doctor flies nearly six hundred miles to sign death certificate. If that was insufficient cause for suspicion, what would it take?

In November, Tina, Georgette and I wrote letters to the medical examiner, Dr. Bruce Levy, and tried to explain why we thought he should exhume our mother's body and perform an autopsy. We didn't know how much he knew about the case. If he only knew what was in the police report, he certainly didn't know enough. He didn't know that she was receiving large quantities of narcotics at various times administered by her husband.

We told him of individuals, such as band members and others in Mom's entourage, who would testify that on more than one occasion Richey had given Mom amounts of medication sufficient to render her unresponsive. Some would testify that she was frequently sedated on the road. Some would testify that they recalled occasions when they heard Mom declining to be given drugs, but they were injected anyway. We told him we were certain that toxicology tests would reveal the presence of powerful narcotics. And we told him that Mom had said several times that she wanted to divorce Richey.

We thought Dr. Levy could order an exhumation and autopsy, but we were wrong. He could only request that the district attorney, Torry Johnson, petition the court for such an order. We were hopeful that he would at least take that step. He didn't. In fact, we never heard from him and our letters did not cause even a small ripple in his office—that is, until the letters turned up in the wrong hands.

Late in December, my sisters and I were stunned to see portions of our letters reprinted in the tabloid *Globe*. They were not written as part of some publicity campaign. We had gone public before and it accomplished nothing. We approached the medical examiner—discreetly, we thought—hoping for complete confidentiality. Instead, our words were screaming from a scandal sheet.

I flinched a little reading them. Those letters were not meant for public consumption. We had been frank in expressing our worst fears, but only so the medical examiner would understand why we were pursuing the autopsy.

How did they find their way to the *Globe*? No one in the medical examiner's office had much interest in finding out what caused our mother's death but maybe someone had an interest in making a fast buck. Tabloids pay for that kind of material.

After the *Globe* story appeared and we voiced our disapproval of the leak, some local reporters had no trouble digging up information. Chris Tassie, a former medical secretary in the ME's office, told a reporter for Channel Five that he had made copies of the letter and claimed others did as well. He admitted approaching Jeny Duke, a columnist for the magazine *Music City News,* who rejected his offer, and he even admitted to bargaining with the *Star*—saying he turned down their offer because it was too low—but he denied selling the letters to the *Globe.*

He apologized for his acts and added, "I want Tammy Wynette's daughters to know that I did not sell those letters to the *Globe* and I didn't sell them to anyone." In response to a question, he said he agreed with our demand for an autopsy.

That was about as far as the case of the purloined letters went, but that was far enough. The incident not only embarrassed the medical examiner, it brought a lot of public pressure on him to reopen the Tammy Wynette case.

Mostly, the crew at Channel Five was responsible for keeping the story alive and in the public eye. Larry Brinton, host of an interview-and-call-in show called *Morning-Line,* devoted a lot of time to the subject. But it was Jennifer Kraus who dug deep and asked the hard questions. She tracked down medical records, court records, forensic experts, lawyers, anyone who could offer an opinion or shed light on the peculiarities of the story.

It was a story that quickly absorbed most of Nashville. People were starting to say, "Yeah, something's not right here."

Jay West, the vice mayor of Nashville, said he wanted an investigation to determine why an autopsy had not been done at the time of death. Kraus interviewed Dr. Cyril Wecht, a prominent pathologist who had investigated such high-profile deaths as those of Elvis Presley, John F. Kennedy, James Earl Ray, David Koresh and JonBenet Ramsey. "I've never heard of a doctor flying in to declare a person dead in this country in modern times," he said.

One television reporter located Sandy Cooper, who had been Mom's housekeeper for a while but had left after a disagreement with Richey. "There's something so wrong with the picture it makes you want to scream," Sandy said. The cameras also sought out country-music stars, most of whom were sympathetic to us. I saw one interview with Ricky Skaggs. He was asked if he thought we were reasonable in our request for an autopsy. "If that happened to my mother, I would want to know. I would *have* to know," he said. Tanya Tucker also supported our autopsy petition and said, "If I found out it was something else I would kick some butt."

Some division in the country-music crowd, in the whole town, was to be expected. Some people calling into Larry Brinton's show accused my sisters and me of acting out of greed, and Dee Jenkins, Conway Twitty's widow, expressed the same view in a television interview. "Where there's a will, there's a relative," she said.

It was understandable that some people would feel that way and there was little we could do except make the perfunctory denials that money was our motive. Sure, we got nothing from Mom's estate, but we were not challenging the will. We were merely trying to find out how our mother died. Proving it was related to drugs, as we believed it was, would not put a penny in our pockets.

What mystified me was that anyone would find it reasonable, in the death of a parent, or any loved one, to accept a cause-of-death diagnosis made by a doctor who was more than five hundred miles away, a doctor who neglected to mention to a police officer that his patient was receiving large doses of narcotics and that the narcotics were at times being administered by a layman.

Most of all, I was mystified that Dr. Bruce Levy could

look at those circumstances and not be a little curious. Why would he not at least call and discuss it with us? Why would he not attempt to find out a little more of what we knew? If he was of the opinion that an exhumation and autopsy were not warranted, fine, but wouldn't he want that opinion to be informed?

Since he was not going to come to us or respond to our letters, we would have to escalate the battle to the next level. The legal level.

Twenty-two

A chorus of country's finest voices fell silent in 1998 . . . Tammy Wynette. Roy Rogers and Gene Autry. Carl Perkins and Eddie Rabbitt and Grandpa Jones and too many others.

While their passings unleashed a torrent of sadness, they also brought out showers of praise and memories of what these performers meant to fans and to country music.

Nowhere was that more evident than in the outpouring of praise for Tammy Wynette, the Mississippi-born superstar who died April 6 of a blood clot.

—COUNTRY WEEKLY, JANUARY 8, 1999

BLOOD CLOT. IT was wrong and I was sure of it and every time I saw it stated as fact, my stomach tightened. Time was hardening it into concrete truth, unchallenged, unquestioned. Somehow, it demeaned my mother's life and her death to attach the wrong explanation to her passing.

* * *

DAN WARLICK WAS ideal.

He was a lawyer with credentials that were of special significance to us. Before coming to Nashville, he had worked for several years in the coroner's office in Memphis, and while he was not trained in forensic pathology, that job had given him a lot of exposure to the workings of a medical examiner's office and to the science of pathology.

We made an appointment with him to discuss our legal options. After listening to our explanations of what we knew about Mom's medications, her relationship with Richey and her close association with Dr. Marsh, Dan began by explaining what we already knew—that we had no legal standing to request an autopsy. But, he said, that did not rule out an autopsy. If the medical examiner could be persuaded by the new information we could give him, he could ask the district attorney to petition for a court order to exhume the body.

Word of her death had reached *The National Enquirer* as early as five-thirty or six o'clock. Richey claimed he found her dead at seven. Although God knows how many people were present at the house, 911 was not called until nearly nine o'clock. Dan Warlick had no trouble seeing the oddities of this scenario.

"Let's set up a meeting with Levy," he said.

Dan contacted him and the meeting was scheduled for Monday, February 8. Finally, it seemed, we were making some headway, but when a story about our crusade appeared in *The Tennessean* on February 6, I developed a strong sense that Levy would not be an easy sell. He told the newspaper that he had no reason to question Marsh's blood-clot conclusion because the doctor was intimately familiar with my mother's condition and medical history.

"It's not an unreasonable diagnosis for him to make," Levy said. "If that was the case, we would have questioned him at the time."

Not unreasonable? What did that mean? It doesn't matter what caused Tammy Wynette's death as long as the doctor made a reasonable guess? No, this did not sound like a guy who would change his mind easily.

The meeting lasted ninety minutes, and throughout Dr. Levy was low-key and attentive—and almost impossible to read. Although her addiction to painkillers had been mentioned in the press for years, he seemed surprised to learn that Mom had been taking strong narcotics regularly at the time of her death.

No one had told him. On the night of April 6, Dr. Marsh had mentioned only antibiotics and anticoagulants to the police officer who reached him by phone. On April 7, Dr. Levy talked by phone with Dr. Marsh, who had arrived in Nashville several hours earlier, and no mention was made of the narcotics. Apparently Marsh, in talking with Levy, repeated what he had told me on April 7—that Mom's weight and vital signs were looking good and she was reasonably healthy.

Therefore, Levy's perspective on the situation was pretty limited: Normal, healthy woman on harmless antibiotics dies suddenly and unexpectedly. Could have been a heart attack. Could have been a blood clot. Highly respected out-of-town surgeon says blood clot, so run with it. Strong narcotics? That puts a different slant on things.

When the meeting ended, I was optimistic. Dr. Levy told us he would review the case and inform us of his decision in a few days. When I read the newspaper the next morning, I was buoyed even further.

The lead paragraph quoted Levy as saying that had he known Tammy Wynette was taking narcotics, he *might* have ordered an autopsy before her body was released to the funeral home. He said that on April 7 Marsh told him "that he'd been treating her for quite some time, that she had a history of clots and that he suspected that is what had happened to her."

But, he added, "Had we known about the medications that she was on at the time of her death, that may have raised questions in our mind about whether an autopsy needed to be held or not."

Reporters also tried to reach Dr. Marsh in Pittsburgh, but he would not grant interviews. Instead, he issued a written statement:

"For six years I had the privilege of serving as Ms. Tammy Wynette's personal physician. She was a person of great dignity and strength. That she had been in poor health was widely known, but the full nature and extent of her illnesses and other debilitating effects were matters she considered private. On this she was adamant, and it is not my intention, even now, to break faith with her wishes.

"However, regarding the cause of death, as the physician most familiar with Ms. Wynette's medical history, my observations and examinations of her at the scene on the evening of her death leave, in my medical opinion, no doubt that her death resulted from the effects of blood clots to her lungs.

"This condition had threatened Ms. Wynette's life several times in the past years, and every indicator on April 6 pointed directly to this as the cause of death. There is no valid reason to suspect any other cause."

Every indicator? What indicators? He had made the diagnosis before he left Pittsburgh for Nashville that night. Did he look for a reason "to suspect any other cause"?

It would have been a simple matter to draw a vial of blood before the body was whisked off to the funeral home to be embalmed. Toxicology tests on the blood could have revealed if there was another possible reason for her death.

ON WEDNESDAY, FEBRUARY 10, Dr. Levy called Dan Warlick to inform him of his decision. He then called a press conference to inform the rest of the world.

Stepping up to a cluster of microphones at a podium outside his office, Levy said:

"I have decided not to ask the district attorney to petition the court to exhume the body of Tammy Wynette. I did not make this decision lightly. After meeting with Miss Wynette's daughters, I decided to conduct a thorough review of this case. I have spoken to Miss Wynette's personal physician and reviewed detailed reports about the nature of Miss Wynette's health, which influenced my decision. I have also reviewed Tennessee law regarding disinterment to perform an autopsy. The purpose of a medical examiner's autopsy is to determine the manner and cause of death from unnatural causes. Based upon review of her medical history, she was terminally ill and her death was due to natural causes. I can find no substantial evidence that it was due to unnatural causes. Her death was not unexpected."

When he opened the press conference for questions, the first was one that was on my lips as soon as I heard his re-

marks: What terminal illness? That was the first I or anyone else had ever heard mention of a terminal illness and I
didn't buy it for a second. If Mom had known she was terminally ill, she would have told us right away. She was private about her illnesses, but only to the extent of wanting
to keep her condition out of the press because of the effect
it might have on her bookings. She didn't try to hide things
from her children. When she discovered a tumor in her
breast, she called Gwen immediately. She often described
one symptom or another to Georgette and asked her to explain it. If she thought she was dying, she would have
gathered her children and grandchildren around her and
kept them there until she was gone.

"What terminal illness did she have?" a reporter asked.

"Miss Wynette preferred to keep a lot of information
about her specific medical condition private," Levy said. "I
could say she was suffering from multiple medical problems, primarily of which are problems with blood clotting.
So, I believe that Dr. Marsh's opinion that death was due to
blood clots is true."

You don't have to have a medical degree to know that a
blood clot doesn't fall into the category of terminal illness.
As Marsh had in his statement a couple of days earlier,
Levy was putting up a rampart that would let him hide
from the incoming questions: Tammy Wynette's desire for
privacy. It was insane. She was dead. Do dead people have
privacy rights? Don't their survivors have a right to know
the cause of death?

Levy said that Dr. Marsh acknowledged prescribing
narcotics for Mom.

"Why didn't he tell you about the drugs last year?"
someone asked.

With a perfectly straight face, Levy said, "He felt that

this was a miscommunication error. He thought the information was relayed through the home health-care nurses
who were helping to care for Miss Wynette and [he] did not
realize at the time that information was not provided to us."

Let's consider that. You're a doctor in Pittsburgh and
you get a call from a police officer in Nashville and he tells
you he is making out his report on your dead patient. Was
she receiving any medication? he asks. You give him a detailed list of innocuous antibiotics and blood thinners, even
the dosages, but you say nothing of the potentially lethal
narcotics because you assume the home nurse has already
supplied that information to the cops. The next day, you
talk on the phone with the medical examiner and, once
again, you neglect to mention the narcotics. Surely the
home nurse has supplied that information.

To my mind, this was more than a "miscommunication
error." It may not have bothered Levy, but it infuriated me,
and from the questioning that followed, it troubled the reporters, too.

Did he not find anything out of the ordinary about the
reporting of Tammy Wynette's death? How could you rule
out respiratory depression? What about the delay in calling
911? Did he not find any of that reason to look at this a little further?

It was then that Levy stopped hiding behind Tammy
Wynette's privacy and tried to hide behind the law, which
turned out to be a flimsy screen. He repeated his opinion
that her death was due to natural causes and, that being the
case, "the law specifically does not allow me to act."

The law does not state that the medical examiner has to
have evidence of an unnatural death, but a "suspicion" is
sufficient to justify an autopsy. In the face of all he now
knew, wasn't Levy even a little suspicious?

Apparently not. The attending physician failed to disclose important information to him and the police. Now the attending physician not only acknowledged prescribing narcotics but may have led the medical examiner to introduce the specter of a terminal illness.

We hadn't won over the medical examiner, but the effort had been more fruitful than I would have guessed.

Dr. Levy revealed that he had received a letter from Dr. Marsh describing the "powerful narcotic therapy" that Mom was receiving and in that letter he noted that her health had taken a sharp turn for the worse in the twenty-four hours before she died. Richey had called him on Sunday afternoon and told him that Mom was in severe pain. Dr. Marsh told him to get her to a hospital immediately. Marsh told Levy that Mom had refused to be admitted, and rather than insisting that she do so, Richey treated her with sedatives and painkillers.

Marsh had made no mention of that when I talked to him the day after Mom died.

Later that evening, after Levy's press conference had been all over the airwaves, Richey again declined to talk with reporters but issued another statement:

"At this point there really is not much to say. Dr. Marsh . . . was never in doubt as to the cause of Tammy's passing and now that has been affirmed by the medical examiner's office. It has been difficult emotionally to deal with these issues the past few days because losing Tammy was more painful than it is possible to describe. Anyone who has lived with and loved another person as I loved her understands what that means. I was blessed to be married to an extraordinary woman. I will miss her always."

* * *

CHANNEL FIVE KEPT hammering at the story. Nashville was quickly polarizing, and shows such as Larry Brinton's attracted eager and opinionated callers. I appeared on one show with Jan Smith and had to take my share of lumps. It was all about money, some people believed, and I could not dissuade them from their thinking.

"The girls seem awfully greedy," one woman allowed. "Why would they want to do this to George Richey?"

Dr. Levy and District Attorney Torry Johnson appeared on another show and they had to take their lumps, too. "The district attorney's not doing his job, the medical examiner's not doing his job and we ought to replace them both," one guy said.

I could handle the criticism and I suppose they could, too.

Twenty-three

IN OUR EFFORTS to get to the truth, we could not have hoped for a stronger investigative journalist than Jennifer Kraus. A lot of people in Nashville, even some of those sympathetic to the questions my sisters and I had raised, may have been willing to shrug off the whole thing, to write off the truth as being forever unknowable.

There were just too many things that didn't add up, but we were inexperienced in digging. Where do you look? What questions do you ask? Which explanations are logical and which are not? We were not detectives. We were determined to know the truth, but we were ignorant of the methods of getting at it.

There were people in Nashville who simply wanted the story to go away, to die a death inflicted by futility and frustration.

It might well have died had it not been for Jennifer Kraus and her colleagues at Channel Five. She kept the searchlight on Richey and Dr. Marsh. She wouldn't let the medical examiner slide by with glib or evasive answers.

And she scoured the public records with an eye for discrepancies—and found plenty of them.

Some of the public documents most critical to our effort, it turned out, were in probate court, where Mom's will was filed and her estate was being settled.

Getting an estate clear for assignment to the heirs can take a long time. It usually involves filing an inventory of the estate—a listing of all the assets—and publishing legal notices to give anyone a chance to contest it or, in the case of debtors, time to file claims against the assets.

In Mom's case, an inventory was not submitted to the probate court, but claims against the estate certainly were.

Jennifer copied those documents and shared them with me.

Georgette was at my house one evening and we sat at the dining table with the papers scattered everywhere.

Mostly they were pretty ordinary: SunTrust Bank of Nashville wanted the $425,000 that was owed on the house at 4916 Franklin Road, plus the $68,793.78 balance of an equity loan against that house. Citicorp Credit Services filed a claim for $35,488—we had no idea what that was for—and a $558,475.64 promissory note from the First National Bank of Malden, Missouri. We assumed that had something to do with the car dealership Mom bought for Richey's brother to run. There were a few smaller claims that appeared to be credit card balances, but none of that really concerned us.

A couple of other items caught our attention then or became important later. One was a bill for $50,954 for Mom's treatment at the University of Pittsburgh Medical Center. Attached to it were several pages of itemized costs.

Then we came to three bills submitted by Care Solutions of Nashville, Inc., which had been providing home health care for Mom since February 1998.

The first was an $8,400 bill for 20 units of "genotropin

5.8 mg Ingra-Mix." That meant nothing to me, but I assumed it was no big deal, since Georgette showed no reaction. We knew Mom was taking a lot of drugs—Valium, Demerol and various other painkillers that she could get her hands on by just about any means.

Georgette tossed that bill aside and looked at the next few pages.

Two shipments of "Versed 5 mg/ml, 1 ml Vial." Twenty units were sent to the house on March 1, 1998, and nine units delivered on April 6, 1998—the day Mom died. Versed became significant later.

"What is Versed?" I asked Georgette when the topic came up later.

"Jackie, this stuff is really dangerous," she said.

"How dangerous?"

After a pause, she said, "Dangerous enough that she shouldn't have been getting it at home."

She tried to explain to me exactly what Versed was, but with no medical training, I couldn't appreciate the gravity of what she was saying.

"Jackie," she insisted, "that is very powerful stuff. It's given to people who are about to undergo a medical procedure. It erases the memory so they will not remember any pain suffered during the procedure. I'm sure it's not supposed to be used outside of a hospital."

If that was true, then why in God's name would a reputable surgeon permit Versed to be used at home? That was preposterous. It couldn't be as dangerous as Georgette believed.

I think even she doubted her knowledge of Versed. She went to the phone and called a friend in Alabama, a nurse she worked with at the hospital.

When she hung up the phone, I could see the anger flashing in her eyes.

"I was right," she said. "This stuff can kill you."

* * *

I BEGAN TO read up on Versed. Georgette understood drugs and medications much better than I, but I was determined to know exactly what it was that was being injected into my mother's veins.

Medical books and references contained some useful information, but it wasn't until I began searching the Internet that I found a lot of information presented in layman's terms that I could understand.

At first, I found the usual dry, clinical descriptions that meant little to me. Versed is a brand name for midazolam hydrochloride, which is one of the chemical class benzodiazepine, a central nervous system depressant, I learned. So what? Valium and Halcion are members of that same group and they seemed to be as common as aspirin.

Then I read that Versed is two and a half times more potent than Valium, and that was the first eye opener. If my mother was in that much pain, she should have been in a hospital.

On a University of Iowa web site, I found this explanation of the drug:

> *Exact mechanism of action is unclear but is similar to that of other drugs in this class. It works to intensify the activity of a major inhibitory neurotransmitter of the brain, producing a feeling of calm and relaxation. Sleep is induced and pain and memory are blocked (which is a fancy way of saying it chemically alters your brain for a brief period of time and then makes you relax and not be afraid, and also, depending on the dose, makes you forget what has happened to you).*
>
> *This medication can be given in a variety of ways: Orally, rectally in a suppository, intranasally in a spray, as an injection in a deep muscle and by injec-*

*tion directly into a vein. IV administration of this drug
is by far the most common route of administration.*

From that, I began to realize that Versed is not purely a
painkiller. That may be one of its effects, but the brain-
altering aspects were overriding. This stuff was used for
something entirely different. Still, it seemed no more pernicious than some of the other drugs I knew Mom had
taken over the years. It sounded relaxing and calming, and
it induced amnesia.

Then I came to the list of possible adverse reactions:
Coughing, pain at the injection site, nausea, vomiting,
headache, blurred vision, fluctuation in vital signs, hypotension, *respiratory depression and respiratory arrest.*
The last two were appalling. If I understood those terms
correctly, this meant that Versed, as Georgette said, could
have killed our mother.

Still, I wasn't sure I was interpreting all of this correctly. Medical terms do not always mean the same thing to
laymen that they mean to doctors, so there was a lot of
room for error on my part.

But there was no comfort in acknowledging my own
limitations in grasping what I was dealing with. At the very
least, I knew that my mother had been given a powerful,
addictive drug that could erase her memory, make her violently ill and weaken her for long periods of time.

Then, at another web site called "informed drug guide"
I found:

*Depending on its dose, midazolam can cause every
stage of a cardiovascular and respiratory depression.
High IV doses have caused cardiac and respiratory
arrest with lethal consequences. Usual doses normally cause a minor decrease of the blood pressure
and oxygen saturation. The amnesia desired for endo-*

*scopies can last much longer than the intervention,
sometimes for hours (semiconsciousness). Occasionally daydreams with sexual content occur. In addition
to a multitude of central nervous symptoms (vertigo,
dizziness, headaches, rarely hallucinations, etc.), midazolam can also cause visual disturbances and nausea. Repeated administration leads to tolerance and
dependence within weeks; withdrawal syndrome often
occurs if the drug is discontinued abruptly.*

Lethal consequences. That was all the confirmation I
needed.

Her doctor was writing prescriptions for a drug that could
kill her, yet he wrote on her death certificate that she died of
a blood clot to the lung, something he could not have known
for certain without an autopsy. And, when he talked later
with the Davidson County medical examiner, convincing
him also that a clot was the cause of her death, he never
mentioned that he had been prescribing Versed for Mom.

I was floored. That seemed to say it all, I believed, but I
was wrong. There was much more to come.

The more I prowled the Internet, the more proficient I
became at tracking down the appropriate web sites. Finally, I landed on the home page of Roche Pharmaceuti-
cals, which markets midazolam under the brand name
Versed, and found another shoe waiting to fall.

That site contained a detailed discussion of Versed beginning with this familiar warning:

*Intravenous Versed has been associated with respi-
ratory depression and respiratory arrest, especially
when used for sedation in noncritical care settings. In
some cases, where this was not recognized promptly
and treated effectively, death or hypoxic encephalopa-*

thy has resulted. Intravenous Versed should be used only in hospital or ambulatory care settings, including physicians' and dental offices, that provide for continuous monitoring of respiratory and cardiac function, i.e., pulse oximetry. Immediate availability of resuscitative drugs and age- and size-appropriate equipment for bag/valve/mask ventilation and intubation, and personnel trained in their use and skilled in airway management should be assured.

The initial intravenous dose for sedation in adult patients may be as little as 1 mg, but should not exceed 2.5 mg in a normal healthy adult. Lower doses are necessary for older (over 60 years) or debilitated patients and in patients receiving concomitant narcotics or other central nervous system depressants. The initial dose and all subsequent doses should always be titrated slowly; administer over at least two minutes and allow an additional two minutes to fully evaluate the sedative effect.

Continuous monitoring by trained personnel. Nothing like that was available to my mother, even though substantial quantities of the drug had been delivered to her house the day she died. And there was more in a section listing the occasions when injectable Versed can be used:

—Intramuscularly or intravenously for preoperative sedation/anxiolysis/amnesia.

—Intravenously as an agent for sedation . . . prior to or during diagnostic, therapeutic or endoscopic procedures, such as bronchoscopy, gastroscopy, cystoscopy, coronary angiography, cardiac catheterization, oncology procedures, radiologic procedures, suture of lacerations and other procedures . . .

—Intravenously for induction of general anesthesia, before administration of other anesthetic agents.

—Continuous intravenous infusion for sedation and tubulated and mechanically ventilated patients as a component of anesthesia or during treatment in a critical care setting.

And there was yet another warning:

Versed must never be used without individualization of dosage, particularly when used with other medications capable of producing central nervous system depression. Prior to the intravenous administration of Versed in any dose, the immediate availability of oxygen, resuscitative drugs, age- and size-appropriate equipment for bag/valve/mask ventilation and intubation, and skilled personnel for the maintenance of a patent airway and support of ventilation should be ensured. Patients should be continuously monitored with some means of detection for early signs of hypoventilation, airway obstruction or apnea, i.e., pulse oximetry. The immediate availability of specific reversal agents (flumazenil) is highly recommended. Vital signs should continue to be monitored during the recovery period.

If I still had doubts about the lethal nature of this drug, the kicker to that warning dissolved them:

Because Versed depresses respiration and because opitoid agonists and other sedatives can add to this depression Versed should be administered . . . only by a person trained in general anesthesia and should be used . . . only in the presence of personnel skilled in early detection of hypoventilation. . . .

Scrolling down the text, I found still another version of that warning, in bold, all-capitalized letters, as though the manufacturer were screaming the message for effect.

> *BECAUSE SERIOUS AND LIFE-THREATENING CARDIORESPIRATORY ADVERSE EVENTS HAVE BEEN REPORTED, PROVISION FOR MONITORING, DETECTION AND CORRECTION OF THESE REACTIONS MUST BE MADE FOR EVERY PATIENT TO WHOM VERSED INJECTION IS ADMINISTERED, REGARDLESS OF AGE OR HEALTH STATUS.*

I don't pretend to have understood everything in that document, but it didn't take a physician to digest the repetitive, boldface warnings.

> *Only in hospital or ambulatory care settings . . . personnel skilled in detection of hypoventilation . . . vital signs should continue to be monitored . . . administered by a person trained in general anesthesia . . .*

Although Mom had a home health-care provider around much of the time, I never saw one of them administer the drugs. Even if the nurse had, it would have been dangerous unless she had been trained in general anesthesia, which was unlikely.

Like just about all of Mom's medications, the Versed was sometimes administered by Richey.

WE WERE NOT detectives, but we knew a marked trail when we saw one. It now seemed more likely that Mom had died from the application of Versed than from a blood clot to the lung. At least, the Versed cast enough doubt on Dr. Marsh's official ruling to warrant an autopsy.

But what was Care Solutions' role in all of this? Why would it deliver to our mother a substance it surely knew was potentially fatal without the proper monitoring equipment and trained personnel to administer it?

Eventually, we found the contract, or consent form, that authorized that company to provide services to Mom. It was dated February 6, 1998, two months before Mom died.

> *I, Tammy Wynette, authorize Care Solutions of Nashville, Inc., to provide medical care to me at home. I understand my treatment was prescribed by my doctor and may be changed by additional doctors' orders. I will participate in my care. Care Solutions of Nashville, Inc., recommends communications between patient and physician.*
>
> *I understand that Care Solutions . . . is not an emergency rescue service and if an emergency occurs, my access and/or transport to a hospital or other facility must be by ambulance service or other parties. Care Solutions will provide treatment to me only during scheduled visits unless an unscheduled visit is arranged. I may need a family member, friend or additional care giver and services to assist with my care between visits.*
>
> *I understand there is no guarantee about the results of my treatment. My physician has explained the benefits and risks of my therapy.*

Having become extremely cynical about everything related to Mom's health care, I read that agreement to mean that Care Solutions was being contracted to deliver drugs prescribed by Dr. Marsh.

All we could do was to keep asking questions. Well, there was one other thing we could do. . . .

Twenty-four

THE CLOCK WAS ticking.

Dan Warlick had advised us that if we were going to take legal action, it would have to be before April 6, 1999, because the statute of limitations for bringing a wrongful-death suit runs out in a year.

There was no doubt in my mind that that was precisely what we wanted to do. We contacted another attorney, Ed Yarbrough, who had more experience in this kind of case, and he agreed to talk with us. We hired him to be our lead attorney if a suit was filed, and Dan Warlick would assist him. Both had valuable, if varying, experience and expertise. Warlick had worked in the Memphis coroner's office—he'd participated in the Elvis Presley autopsy—so he knew the inner workings of such a place, but Ed had more trial experience. We wanted both.

At first, Ed was the more cautious one, probably because he was still familiarizing himself with the facts of the case. Accusing someone of wrongfully causing the death of another person is not a step to be taken casually, particularly when one of those likely to be accused is the widower of the deceased person and the other is a renowned transplant specialist.

After becoming even cursorily acquainted with the circumstances surrounding my mother's death, Ed believed something was amiss. He had studied the drug list we supplied him with and he thought that if Mom was taking certain ones of them in combination with certain others, the results could have been fatal. Versed and Phenergan is just one example of a potentially dangerous pairing. Both were on her list of medications, but we had no way of knowing if they were administered in tandem or in what quantities.

According to what he knew, he thought there might be a case against Dr. Marsh, but a case against Richey would be more difficult. He wasn't a doctor, so he couldn't be accused of medical malpractice. If he had done nothing but follow the doctor's instructions in administering medication, he could be found blameless. And Marsh had imposing credentials. From the University of Arkansas to residency in Dallas to a fellowship at the august Mayo Clinic, he was on the ascending fast track early. He turned a fellowship at the University of Pittsburgh into a position as a surgeon and then moved to Washington University Medical Center in St. Louis to head up the liver-transplant program, later returning to Pittsburgh.

The clock was ticking.

There was a lot to consider before going into court. Lawsuits against doctors are difficult because it is hard to find other doctors willing to testify against them. There was a time when the courts recognized—perhaps they still do—the *conspiracy of silence* within the medical community. Judges in malpractice cases routinely told juries they could take that *conspiracy* into account when weighing the evidence in a case.

Ed had a lot besides that to weigh and he was doing just that at the end of March when he got an unexpected call from a lawyer friend of his who lived in Knoxville. Bob Ritchie, his friend, was representing Dr. Wallis Marsh.

He told Ed that he was in Nashville with Marsh and William Manifesto, Marsh's personal attorney in Pittsburgh. They would like to come by and talk. Ed was bowled over by the suggestion. Not often does a defendant in a case he is about to file want to talk to him. It offered interesting possibilities.

He invited them to come to his office at five o'clock and then he called Dan Warlick to invite him to the meeting.

After the usual introductions, Ed escorted everyone into a conference room with a long meeting table. When they were seated, Dr. Marsh began to pull documents from a large file he had brought with him. It appeared that Mom's entire medical history was there, including X rays. Ed realized that Dr. Marsh and his lawyers thought that by presenting their case to Ed, they could head off a lawsuit.

If that was the case, the strategy backfired in a big way—largely because they were unaware of Dan's credentials in pathology.

Ed told me later that Marsh's presentation might have overwhelmed him, but not Dan.

For three hours, they sat in the conference room courtroom, with Marsh offering an explanation and Dan Warlick cross-examining him. The result, Ed said, was that the visit bolstered the case for a wrongful-death suit. Marsh had prescribed the portable catheter and the long-term drug use. Both could be implicated in a blood clot (until it was proved that a blood clot was not the cause, Ed had to proceed on that basis).

"That provided us with the legal theory that Dr. Marsh, in effect, harmed his patient by his course of treatment," Ed said.

But was it enough? As the meeting wore on, Ed grew confident that a lawsuit was justified. That decision was sealed near the end of the meeting, when Marsh discussed his telephone conversation with Richey the day before Mom died. Richey had called and told him Mom was complaining of numbness in her legs and described other symptoms that suggested a blood clot. He urged Richey to get Mom to the hospital, where she could be treated for a possible blood clot. For whatever reason, Richey did not do that.

"Are you saying, then, that if George Richey had taken Tammy to the hospital that night when you told him to that she would have lived?" Ed asked him.

"Yes," Marsh replied.

Not only had Marsh implicated himself by opening up Mom's medical history, he had just told my attorney that but for the failure of Richey to follow his medical advice, Tammy Wynette would not have died.

The suit was filed on April 5, one day before the statute of limitations would have run out. It named Wallis Marsh and George Richey as defendants and asked for $50 million in damages.

It was a long list of allegations, based on everything we had been able to determine about the behavior of both men.

In summary, we charged that Dr. Marsh had been negligent in his treatment of my mother, and contributed to her wrongful death, by maintaining her "on a regimen of narcotic and other addictive prescription medicine," by "attempt[ing] to be [Mom's] primary physician . . . when he lived in excess of five hundred miles away from her," and by failing to refer Mom to local doctors who were available to treat her pain and narcotic addiction.

When the suit was first filed we also named Richey as a co-defendant and complained that he had "improperly maintained [Mom's] narcotic addiction, improperly administered narcotics to her and failed to see that she would receive emergency medical treatment at a time when he could have, and should have, known that failure to do so would, or could, result in her death."

That was it. Everything said.

I must admit that my satisfaction at getting the matter into court was dulled by the fact that the lawsuit didn't necessarily advance the cause of an autopsy. And there was one other thing that Ed Yarbrough had explained to us.

If we won the suit, Richey would also be a winner, of sorts. As Tammy Wynette's widower, under Tennessee law, he would be entitled to one-third of any damages the jury awarded. Whether he could actually collect any money was unclear—a lot of circumstances would have to be factored in—but the possibility existed.

Also, I knew that some people would take the lawsuit and the $50 million it asked for as proof that Tammy Wynette's daughters were only in this fight for the money. The fact of life and law is that monetary damages have to be a part of a civil action or the action is meaningless. You have to affix a dollar amount or the other side has no reason to so much as respond to your allegations.

RICHEY WAS SILENT, but a couple of days later, his lawyers released a statement to the press.

"George Richey devoted his life to caring for Tammy. In the latter years, her treatment included extraordinary medical care from a team of physicians at the University of Pittsburgh Medical Center. The medical care that she received from Dr. Marsh and his team, and the loving care she received from George Richey, together extended her life and permitted her to do what she loved. All this recent publicity is particularly distressing given Tammy's longstanding wish that her medical treatments be kept private and confidential. All of these allegations are totally false, without foundation, and that will be proven in a court of law."

To me, the statement contained all the predictable signals that Richey and Marsh remained united in their defense and were sticking to their "loving care" story.

Yet something was going on that I couldn't readily detect. There was the usual media feeding frenzy, and with Richey refusing to meet with reporters, the slant was mostly from our side.

This time Richey was no longer trying to manipulate the press. He just wanted it to go away.

A reporter and photographer from the London *Sunday Times* magazine came to town and spent a lot of time with me and my sisters, our lawyers and anyone else who would talk to them. They put together one of the most balanced, thoroughly researched and best-written accounts that had been published. They tried to interview Richey, but he declined.

One afternoon, Georgette accompanied the magazine's photographer to the house where Mom had lived. Shortly after Mom died, Richey had an iron gate placed across the driveway, so the photographer had to shoot whatever he could see from the street. He was not trespassing.

Richey approached him and said, "What do you want, asshole?"

The photographer asked him if he could photograph any memorabilia of Mom that might be available.

"I have all the stuff," Richey scowled. "No one else has anything. I have all Tammy's stuff locked up in the house. No one will see it. It's mine and no one else has any . . . I don't want to see you again, asshole."

The pressure was building.

ABOUT NINE O'CLOCK on the morning of Wednesday, April 14, eight days after we filed the lawsuit, Ed Yarbrough called me at work.

"Are you sitting down?" he asked, a question that told me he had heavy-duty news.

"Yes. Why?"

"I just got a fax from Richey's lawyer and he's agreed to an autopsy," Ed said.

"Great," I said. "So when do we expect it? Within a couple of days?"

"It's happening now," he said.

Twenty-five

I WAS A little unprepared for it to get under way so fast.

"Can you call your sisters?" Ed asked. "I don't have time. I'm on my way to the coroner's office."

"What about Dan?"

"I've located him. He's in court in Lebanon, but he's been notified and he's on his way."

There was one other person I was curious about. Dr. Charles Harlan. He was a distinguished and acclaimed pathologist who had been Davidson County medical examiner from 1983 to 1993 and was now the consulting forensic pathologist for the state of Tennessee. We had made it clear to our lawyers that if an autopsy was performed, we wanted someone representing us to be present. Bruce Levy had given us no reason to rely solely on his judgment. Our attorneys had talked to Dr. Harlan and he agreed to be our observer when and if an autopsy was ordered.

We had also advised Bruce Levy of those wishes when we met with him in February. "That's fine," he assured us.

Was Dr. Harlan notified? Was he there? Ed was already off the phone before I could ask.

I called Martha Dettwiller. "I'm going to the coroner's office," I told her. "Wanna go with me?"

She was as excited as I. If Dr. Harlan witnessed the autopsy, we would, at last, be getting some long-sought answers. "Let's go," she said.

We drove into downtown, found 84 Hermitage Avenue and pulled into the parking lot. I was extremely uncomfortable, fearing that I might run into Richey or that the place would be some kind of media mob scene. Instead, there was almost no sign of activity. The only other people we saw were two men sitting in a car across the lot from us.

It felt strange sitting there, almost as though we were interlopers. We wondered if it would be appropriate for us to go inside. What purpose would that serve? No one was going to tell us anything. I looked for Richey's car and didn't see it. Where were my attorneys?

After about ten minutes, the two men got out of their car and walked toward us. When they reached our car, I rolled down the window. One of them told us they were with Channel Two. "Are you here in connection with the Tammy Wynette autopsy?" His eyes went from me to Martha and back again.

"No," I said. The last thing I wanted now was another television interview.

"Do you know anything about it?" I think he recognized me, or thought he did, which would not have been unusual. In the past few weeks, my sisters and I had been on television more than Barbara Walters.

"No," I said, wishing he would go away.

"Well . . . we got word of it, you know . . . and we're trying to confirm it," he said, obviously trying to keep the conversation going until we admitted something.

"Don't know anything," I said.

They went back to their car and a few minutes later we saw Jennifer Kraus and her crew drive up. Not wanting to get caught in the crossfire of cameras, Martha and I drove out of the lot and found a parking place across the street and waited there. In just a short time, we saw the news vehicles and a few other cars leaving, so we assumed it was all over.

RICHEY HAD ABRUPTLY authorized the autopsy the day before and the medical examiner wasted no time. Just after daybreak, workers at the mausoleum, working with just a screwdriver, removed the brass screws from the marble slab across the front of Mom's vault, slid the coffin out and loaded it into a hearse.

By eight o'clock, the autopsy was under way. This was what I had wanted. This was what we had waged a long and public battle for. But I felt no joy at knowing what was happening inside the medical examiner's laboratory. An autopsy is not a gentle procedure, but I kept telling myself, *That's not Mom in there, that's just the remains of a woman who is in a better place now.* And then I tried not to think about it.

We drove back to Martha's house. I called Ed Yarbrough's office, but he was still out. It was well after noon before I talked to Dan Warlick.

He told me that Mom's body was returned to the tomb

at one o'clock and that the medical examiner would not have results for a while.

"Was Dr. Harlan there?" I asked.

"He sure was," Dan said. "When I found out they were doing it this morning, I told Levy he'd better not start until we got there."

"How long before we know something?" I asked.

"Four weeks, maybe five," he said. An eternity.

The airwaves were jumping with the news. Richey's unexpected reversal had caught everyone by surprise. He had been implacable in his refusal to approve an autopsy, and it escaped no one's notice that his change of heart came in close proximity—one week and change—of being named in a wrongful-death lawsuit.

After Mom was back in her tomb, Richey called a press conference at the Doubletree Hotel in downtown Nashville.

This time he read his prepared statement instead of issuing it through his lawyers, and he read it in a voice laced with anger and bitterness. This is what he said:

"Yesterday, I requested that an autopsy be performed on my late wife, Tammy Wynette. It is my understanding that the autopsy has been completed and that her body has been returned to its resting place at the Woodlawn Mausoleum. It is my hope that this autopsy will clarify for everyone how Tammy died so we can all move on. Tammy was a woman who knew what she wanted in life and in death. She made it clear to me, to her physician, to some of her family members and her friends that she had two wishes if she preceded me in death. First, she did not want her body to be cremated and secondly, she did not want there to be an autopsy on her body.

"I knew Tammy for twenty-eight years plus. She cared for other people. She was a very generous, giving and loving woman. I know that she would be willing to pay this price, this intrusion into her privacy, to help end the pain to which I, my family and Tammy's longtime physician and friend have been subjected in recent months.

"Tammy was an extremely strong person, perhaps the strongest person I have ever known. She would have had to be extremely strong emotionally and physically to endure the pain and medical problems that plagued her for years. In fact, to say, as some have, that Tammy didn't make her own decisions or somehow lost control of her life at the end is to insult the memory of this great lady.

"In her later years, as her condition worsened, Tammy chose to work with renowned surgeon Dr. Wallis Marsh and his team of physicians at the University of Pittsburgh Medical Center. I am very grateful for the excellent care that she received from Dr. Marsh and his staff. He is a compassionate, professional and very talented surgeon who became a personal friend, giving her unsurpassed care. I deeply regret that the fine care from Dr. Marsh has been questioned in recent months.

"I'm saddened, too, by the lawsuits filed by Tammy's daughters. I'm saddened they now question my love and devotion to their mother. They truly know better. I'm saddened they have questioned Dr. Marsh. I'm profoundly saddened that her children are now willing to drag their mother's closely guarded private life into the public, leaving me no choice but to respond.

"I'm saddened that out of frustration over financial matters, the daughters have been willing to work so hard to discredit their mother, and that's what they have done. I'm very saddened that part of Tammy's legacy is this fiasco.

"In 1962, I worked in a mortuary as a side job in Tucson, Arizona. I considered that work to be a final service to people on their way to a better place. While I was there, I observed perhaps as many as twenty autopsies. What I saw was not pretty. It's a violent act. It's a violation of who that person was. I know exactly what's happened to Tammy today and I despise it.

"But I'm totally confident about things as well. I'm confident about the resolution of these ridiculous charges. I'm confident about the care provided by Dr. Marsh and his team of physicians. And I know about the love, devotion and care I gave Tammy for over twenty wonderful years.

"It is my hope today puts us one day closer to a peaceful rest for my wife, Tammy. Thank you."

The comments about me and my sisters did not affect me. We had taken our shots at him and, frankly, had expected some return fire long before now.

Richey turned and left the podium and Sylvia stepped forward to answer questions, which seemed to frustrate the reporters.

"Why won't Mr. Richey answer questions?" one of them asked.

"He's a defendant in a civil suit," she said.

Sylvia told the press that on the Sunday before she died, Mom had complained of, among other things, a stinging sensation in the area of her catheter. *Here we go again,* I thought, *reinforcing the theory of the catheter which caused the blood clot which caused the death.* She said that when Richey told Mom that Dr. Marsh wanted her to be hospitalized, Mom said, "You know, I'm feeling so much better, I don't think I'm going to go there. I'm going to stay right here at home."

It was believable that Mom didn't want to go to the hospital. She had been to too many and she hated them. What I found unacceptable was that Richey, knowing her condition, and by then presumably knowing that catheters and blood clots go hand in hand, didn't insist.

IN THE FIRST few days after the autopsy, time seemed to stand still. Until the medical examiner released his findings, I could only wait to hear from my lawyers.

The lawyers, on the other hand, had plenty to do. Richey filed a motion in court asking the judge to dismiss the suit against him on the grounds that as a non-doctor, he couldn't be sued for medical malpractice. I didn't know it at the time, but Ed Yarbrough and Dan Warlick were considering dropping Richey as a defendant and were discussing that with his attorneys.

Nothing, however, would happen until we had the autopsy results.

Jennifer Kraus kept up her tireless digging and somehow found a source, probably someone in the medical examiner's office, who told her that Levy had found no evidence of a blood clot. It wasn't official, but it was solid enough for Jennifer to put on the air.

She, like the rest of us, was never convinced of the blood-clot theory and believed that drugs were the more likely cause.

She called Torry Johnson, the district attorney, and asked the logical question: If it turns out that the Versed killed Tammy Wynette, would he take any action?

Johnson's reply: "No."

The implications of that answer were overwhelming. *If* the district attorney of Davidson County had a case in which a woman incapable of administering drugs to herself died of drug-related causes, he would see no reason to investigate.

Johnson wouldn't budge, but what about Levy? If Jennifer's source was correct and no blood clot had been found in the lung, where would that leave him? If Versed were found in her blood, would he find a way to dismiss that? I was beginning to wonder if this had all been a waste of time.

This is a 55-year-old white female with a complex medical history, including intestinal dysmotility with nutritional deficiency and multiple episodes of thromboembolic disease. She is state-post multiple abdominal surgical procedures and has an indwelling catheter placed for chronic pain management and nutritional support. She expired on April 6, 1998, at her residence in Nashville. The death was reported to the Metro Medical Examiner's Office, and based upon information provided that evening, jurisdiction was declined. Approximately one year later, the deceased's widower requested . . . an autopsy to resolve lingering questions regarding the cause of her death.

The autopsy was performed April 14, 1999. Specimens were obtained for toxicology studies and simultaneously tested at three separate laboratories. The toxicology was qualitatively positive for the presence of midazolam (Versed) and promethazine (Phenergan). None of the laboratories was able to detect the presence of hydromorphone (Dilaudid). Histology specimens were examined and revealed

*multiple old pulmonary emboli with recanalization.
No acute thromboemboli [fatal blood clots] were
identified grossly or microscopically. There was pulmonary hypertension with right ventricular dilation
and hypertrophy secondary to the old emboli.*

*In my opinion, the woman died as a result of
right-side heart failure. The mechanism of her death
is cardiac arrhythmia. The relative contributions to
her death from the underlying natural diseases and
the medications present in her body at the time of her
death cannot be ascertained. Therefore, the manner
of her death cannot be determined.*

So wrote Dr. Levy in the "Summary of Case" at the end
of his autopsy report that was released on May 20.

On the preceding page, under the heading "Cardiovascular System," he had written:

*The 350 gram heart has a smooth, glistening, in-
tact epicardial surface. The coronary arteries are
free of significant atherosclerosis. The myocardium
is homogeneous red-brown without focal lesions.
The left and right ventricles are 1.0 and 0.2 cm. in
thickness at the lateral walls respectively. The right
ventricle is markedly dilated. The left ventrical, right
atrium and left atrium are normal in size. . . .*

That was it? He didn't say she died from a heart attack,
but from "heart failure" brought on by "cardiac arrhythmia." Arrhythmia is an irregular heartbeat, a heartbeat
lacking rhythm. Was he saying merely that she died because her heart stopped beating?

At his press conference, he tried to elaborate.

"These previous blood clots significantly compromised the arteries in her lungs, causing pressure on the right side of her heart as the heart tried to pump blood through these obstructions," he said. "As a result, the right side of the heart was damaged and enlarged, causing the fatal arrhythmia."

What about the presence of the two drugs, which I was told could be lethal when taken together? We knew that because so much time had passed since the embalming, it would be impossible to determine the levels of drugs in her system at the time of death, but didn't the presence of these two suggest something?

"The role that these medications have played is still a question and will probably always be a question. Given that, there will be people who come down with opinions on all sides of that issue," he said.

And what of the mysterious "terminal illness" that had been hoisted as a convenient shield just a few weeks earlier? That vague reference had infuriated me because it refueled some of the AIDS rumors that had circulated for a while. By floating that tidbit and then refusing to identify the illness or disease, the impression was created that my mother had contracted something too horrible to disclose.

Well, Levy conceded, there was no terminal disease, but as if to cover his tracks, he added, "But she had a lot of things wrong with her and her death was not unexpected." If she had not died from the arrhythmia, he said, a clot would have killed her soon.

His audacity was astonishing. First, he relied on Marsh's blood-clot diagnosis and defended it even after learning that Marsh had failed to disclose important information about drugs Mom was receiving. Then, when forced to rescind the blood-clot finding, he advanced the inscrutable argument that *well, if a blood clot didn't kill her, it would have.*

That wasn't quite the end of it.

There was still Dr. Charles Harlan.

He agreed that Mom died of sudden heart failure. But, he said, "Everybody has cardiac arrhythmia when they die of heart failure. It's meaningless. If you die when you're 160 years old, you still die of cardiac arrhythmia."

What caused her heart to stop beating?

"There was no anatomical disease process sufficient to cause her death," he said, challenging Levy's other major conclusion. "There is absolutely no evidence of pulmonary hypertension. The heart is not enlarged. There's no thickening of the pulmonary arteries. There's nothing to support the diagnosis of pulmonary hypertension."

Dr. Harlan also told us that Dr. Levy could have taken photographs of the heart to support his diagnosis—something that is commonly done in contentious autopsies—but he chose not to do so.

Did the drugs cause her death?

"In my opinion, they played a significant role in the cause of her death, but the exact amount of that cannot be determined because we do not have samples of blood, urine or other body fluids taken before embalming," he said. "That was not my responsibility. That was somebody else's responsibility."

It was Bruce Levy's responsibility.

One writer noted in his article about the autopsy that the whole affair may have accomplished nothing, except to deepen the mystery of Tammy Wynette's death. The cause of death entered on the death certificate by Dr. Marsh was shown to be wrong, leaving the real cause to be debated by two experienced pathologists.

For me, the mystery no longer exists. Of the two "experienced pathologists," I considered Dr. Harlan to be by far the more accomplished and more objective.

Even Dr. Levy later went beyond the infuriatingly narrow findings of his autopsy and supported my beliefs on two key points:

Before a national audience on the *Today* show, Levy said that on the night of my mother's death, "the family and Dr. Marsh provided incomplete information to [him] regarding what medication she was on." Levy was very clear: "[H]ad we known about the Versed and the other medication she was on that evening, we would have obtained a blood sample and gotten those exact blood levels."

Levy also made clear that he was not rejecting the possibility that drugs played a role in Mom's death. To the contrary, Levy admitted:

> *There's a definite possibility that those medications [Versed and Phenergan] could have contributed to her death. . . . Versed is a very powerful drug . . . and it . . . can cause respiratory depression and respiratory arrest . . . whether properly or improperly administered.*

From all of this, I am convinced that I have found the answer to the one question I'd had from the outset. I can only conclude from these facts and findings that my mother died, as I had feared, because of the powerful drugs she received.

* * *

IT WAS NOT easy for my sisters and me to agree to it, but, after consulting with our lawyers, we dropped Richey from the wrongful-death suit. In exchange, Richey agreed to surrender his one-third right to any damages we collected and, just as important, to cooperate with our lawyers as they prosecuted the suit against Dr. Marsh.

IN MATTERS SUCH as these, the civil-court system moves torturously slowly. At Dr. Marsh's request, the case was moved to federal court. Focusing on the responsibility of Mom's health-care providers, an amended complaint was filed adding a claim against Care Solutions of Nashville, Inc., the company that had been providing home health care and related services to Mom. With the case now pending against Care Solutions and Dr. Marsh, our lawyers then settled into that agonizing process of filing motions and taking depositions and interviewing expert witnesses and sifting over and over through the mountains of documents and other materials that are accumulated in a lawsuit of this nature.

The story keeps popping back into the news, and our days are still tense with anticipation of everything that is yet to come.

Recently, Richey went to the media to defend his conduct during Mom's last days and after her death. In a *20/20* interview he denied having anything to do with Mom's death, denied arranging for Dr. Marsh to come to Nashville to sign Mom's death certificate, denied having anything to do with the removal of Mom's pain medications from the house after she died.

One day, my daughter embraced me and asked in a forlorn tone that I well understood, "Mom, when is it going to be over?"

For her, soon, I hope. For me, and probably for my sisters, never.

Postscript

ABOUT A WEEK after my mother was buried, I went to a movie theater to see *City of Angels,* a love story in which the female lead, played by Meg Ryan, dies. During her death scene, the background music is a song called "Angel" sung by Sarah McLachlan. The lyrics are about being in the "arms of an angel, far away from here."

I began thinking about my mother. The tears that had never come at that memorial service at the Ryman Auditorium began to flow. I was shaking and limp—not as a result of anything that was happening on screen.

As soon as the movie ended, I hurried outside and stood by my car, breathing the cool spring air. I realized then that I missed my mother more than I had imagined I would. I had grown up with her absences, but in more recent years, when her career became less time-consuming, we had become much closer. I'd gotten along without her for so long as a child that it never occurred to me I would miss her so much as an adult.

I unlocked my car door and slid into the driver's seat. When I turned on the ignition, the radio leapt to life right in the middle of the chorus of Sarah McLachlan's "Angel," the same part that had brought tears during the movie. In the quiet and stillness of my car, it was as though the song were being sung by a thousand voices in a grand cathedral, voices that saturated the air, making me tingle.

It made me emotional all over again, but instead of feeling sad, I found myself smiling. It was as if my mother had sent me this reprise—her way of telling me, "It's okay, I'm in the arms of an angel now."

To this day, every time I hear that song, it reminds me of my mother. My eyes brim with tears, but I'm filled with that same peace, not grief.

Leaving the theater that day, I drove into the twilight toward my home in Brentwood, only to make an impulsive exit from the interstate, drawn by thoughts of my mother to the mausoleum where she lay. I parked and went in the front door, turned left, then made a quick right and ascended the few steps to the long corridor leading to her crypt. I touched the cold marble that separated us and studied the cards and notes that had been left for her. I wanted to write my own words for her, but I couldn't. Not that day, anyway.